The Love of Devotion

Love and Devotion (Book 2)

Donna Goddard

Also by Donna Goddard

Fiction

Waldmeer (Book 1 of Waldmeer)

Together (Book 2 of Waldmeer)

Circles of Separation (Book 3 of Waldmeer)

Faith (Book 4 of Waldmeer)

Pittown (Book 5 of Waldmeer)

Prana (Book 6 of Waldmeer)

Purnima (Book 7 of Waldmeer)

Nonfiction

The Love of Being Loving (Book 1 of Love and Devotion)

The Love of Devotion (Book 2 of Love and Devotion)

Love's Longing (Book 3 of Love and Devotion)

Touched by Love (Book 4 of Love and Devotion)

Dance: A Spiritual Affair (Book 1 of The Creative Spirit Series)

Writing: A Spiritual Voice (Book 2 of The Creative Spirit Series)

Strange Words: Poems and Prayers (Book 3 of The Creative Spirit Series)

Contents

Introduction

The Love of Devotion is the result of several decades of spiritual work. It began the day I first opened the metaphysical door and stepped into a world only minimally understood, at the time, but strongly desired. Metaphysics is concerned with the ultimate, primary, inner aspects of existence. It does not see life in material terms but sees life in terms of thought, and has a strong emphasis on healing.

Everyone's greatest need is for the healing and wholeness that spiritual awareness brings. However, we are often reluctant to commit to it. As Thomas Hora said, "It's easy to be enlightened. It's just not easy to be interested in it." We eventually must come to the realisation that the purpose of our life is to align with our spiritual nature. Try as we do to find other options, there are no viable alternatives that will withstand the inevitable consequences of misplaced loyalties and loves. It is the way for us to find our soul home.

The Love of Devotion is an individual journey, but the struggles and lessons of one person are fundamentally those of all mankind. It is the second book in the series *Love and Devotion* and is largely set within the framework of Devotional Nonduality and the teachings of Dr David R. Hawkins.

As students of life, we seek both relief from suffering and growth of happiness. Deeply considering uplifting ideas raises our consciousness from the realm of the material problem into the powerful and harmonious realm of the spiritual. It is what a dedicated spiritual practice is all about. We give up our own ideas, hurts, fears, and grudges and concede to the Greater. We expand and we heal.

It becomes apparent that it would be impossible to feel alone as we are intimately connected to a thriving life-force. It is everything, yet it is nothing. It grows silently and steadily. We are already it and It is already us. We continue to go forward with our spiritual practices and these practices increasingly envelop us in loveliness. We come out the other side as a transparent being; nameless but with the mark of God.

This edition of *The Love of Devotion* includes quotes, at the end of each chapter, that were in the original edition and were meaningful to me at the time of writing.

Love and Devotion Series

Love and Devotion is a four-book nonfiction series. To find the great Love, we must, one way or another, die the great death. Once that death is conquered, we won't have to die again. There is a grand and magnificent truth that radiates from within all of life and each of us. May you discover in your heart a sweet lightness, the luminescent glow of God's beauty, and a true appreciation for the wonderful gift of life which glows unmarred through every human error. We are loved by the Divine, loved into existence. That, in itself, is enough to reassure each one of us of our inestimable worth.

The first book, of the series, is *The Love of Being Loving*. It is about the earlier adult years of my spiritual development. Dr Thomas Hora (Metapsychiatry) and Mary Baker Eddy (Christian Science) were the most significant influences on my spiritual path during my twenties and thirties.

The second book is *The Love of Devotion*. In my forties, I started reading a series of metaphysical books by Dr David R. Hawkins. I realised that they were having a potent impact on my growth and Dr Hawkins became my next spiritual teacher. Dr Hawkins (Devotional Nonduality) and Dr Hora came from very similar spiritual and intellectual terrain. We are drawn to a certain field of truth that resonates with our inner leanings. My interest in understanding thought drew me to teachers who also had a deep interest in human consciousness.

The third book is *Love's Longing*. Somewhere along the way, there develops within the soul a yearning that can no longer be ignored; a craving for the great Love affair.

The fourth book is *Touched by Love* which is about our body, relationships, and the spiritual path. It is vital to maintain, understand, and balance each of them. We must strengthen, expand, and extend all the energetic systems of our being. It takes work and commitment, but that is the purpose of life.

Chapter 1

In Search of Truth

The Nature of Spiritual Teachers

Existential Crisis

Themuch fruits of serious spiritual devotion have an unmistakable flavour, sometimes even more so in retrospect. It had been a challenging few years. I was twenty-six and had been progressing through an existential crisis; an involuntary falling apart of life's meaning. I felt a deep human aloneness and with all my praying, I failed to feel the love of God in any way which could help my state of being. Other than the care and protection of my two little children and my spiritual studies, I had no interest in anything. Everything seemed trite to me; meaningless and often painfully intolerable. I had lost faith in everything human to give solace to my soul. It was not intentional. It is simply what happened over the space of a few years. I was at the bottom of the valley – all things lost but nothing gained.

What else could I do but pray? Only God could rescue me. I did not doubt that God would do so, but first it seemed that all would be taken away so that new ground would be available for working with. One morning, during the earlier years of this struggle, I was walking along a path at a quiet beach near where we lived. I had my toddler in a stroller and my baby in a tie-on carrier. It was a beautiful suburb in seaside Sydney and all the more beautiful for the glorious day. However, try as I did, none of this had any ability to lift my spirits.

Breath of God

The preceding few days had been particularly difficult. Even the tiny bit of hope I was given after prayer seemed to have disappeared. Tears of grief and despair were my increasingly constant companion, though I knew not what I grieved. Much later, I realised it was the necessary grieving that accompanies the loosening of the hold that the ego has over our consciousness. It is the inevitable struggle of being born human, and yet the soul seeks release from the bondage of thought that constantly revolves around the precious one – ourselves. We grow up trying to develop enough of an ego to be able to survive and thrive in the world. That, in itself, is a mighty effort. Even before we have it mastered, the deeper Self starts speaking to us, whis-pering in our ear that this life is not enough. Then we, almost without noticing, begin the quest of pulling apart the ego that we, so courageously, tried to build.

Having no other option but to go forward, I was walking along the beach boardwalk with my little ones hoping that the natural beauty would, even marginally, rescue me. After a while, I must have forgotten about myself. I was looking out to sea and the grandness of it all caught my attention. I simply forgot, for a moment, to feel so bad. That was the chance. And given the chance, *It* came rushing in. It was so brief that it was over before I even noticed it. But there it was, nevertheless, unmistakable. It came like an invisible breeze brushing past me, coming from the sea, returning beyond, into the Infinite. It wasn't a breeze. It was the breath of God.

As soon as it went, I called internally, *"No, stop! Come back. I have been trying to find you. Stay with me. I need you."*

I knew it was the Divine by the lightness it brought. It was a sweet presence, softening the mind. It was a very welcome breath of fresh air. It could not stay, at that time, but it would later return and become a progressively more comfortable acquaintance. The veil was beginning to part.

Past Teachers

Several decades passed and I continued down the path of awakening. My first book, *The Love of Being Loving*, speaks of these years. One never forgets one's past teachers or disciplines. In my case, Metapsychiatry (and its founder, Dr Thomas Hora) and Christian Science had been my main spiritual influences. Such allegiances are forever enshrined in our heart and continue to help, inspire, and mould us. They are pivotal to our development and our total and absolute devotion to them secures the progress which blossoms from that commitment.

The cemented bond between teacher and student surpasses time and space, and the love of a teacher can be beckoned whenever requested. Further, one often has an ongoing commitment to the other students of a teacher and, indeed, the entire group of that pathway. Nevertheless, in spite of loyalties, our inner spiritual drive will take its own path through the terrain it determines is best. It will have its own timing and will guide us to whoever is most beneficial to the next stage of our growth.

Like Attracts Like

I started reading a series of metaphysical books by Dr David R. Hawkins which began to have a significant impact on my spiritual growth. Dr Hawkins' focus was on the concepts of not juicing the ego, going into an energy field and riding it out, surrender, humility, devotion, and love for everyone and everything, including oneself, at all times. Dr Hawkins and Dr Hora, although appearing at quite different times in my life and with no conscious connection one-to-the-other, came from very similar terrain. We are drawn to a certain field of spiritual truth which resonates with our own inner tendencies and interests. My interest in understanding human consciousness has drawn me to teachers who, themselves, have had a deep interest in human consciousness.

Physicians of the Soul

During the early careers of Hora and Hawkins, New York was a fermenting place of much that was original, brilliant, and challenging in terms of therapy, analysis, and the understanding of the human mind. It is, thus, not surprising that from this fertile and creative ground came dedicated practitioners of mental health who later became dedicated practitioners of spiritual health. Both shared many of the same interests: Zen Buddhism, Taoism, the Christian mystics, existential philosophy, theosophy, Freudian and Jungian analysis, quantum physics, and a profound appreciation of the literature relating to spirituality, healing, consciousness, and nonduality.

Nonduality

Nonduality is a term which reflects devotion to and love of a spiritual Good which has no opposite. It is a realisation of the tremendous power of the invisible life-force of the Divine. God and man are not seen as separate entities, but as One. Both are held with an attitude of devotional love and this devotion unfolds as a sincere and unrelenting walk towards greater self-realisation. The concept of nondualism is originally derived from the sacred texts of the *Upanishads*. It finds its source in the Advaita Vedanta tradition of the Hindu philosophy. It is a system of thought which sees the essence of the human soul as indistinguishable from the Absolute. Nonduality does not make sense to the human mind. It is illogical and goes against everything we sense with our human capacities. One has to open the door to a different realm, and then one begins to experientially and spiritually feel it. Understanding nonduality leads naturally to healing because life is seen in a way that is spontaneously elevating.

All the schools of thought that I have seriously studied are based on an understanding of Reality as being nondualistic.

> *There is only one Life.*
> *Life is good and only good.*
> *Life is freely available to everyone.*

Metaphysics sees life from the perspective of spiritual reality. By praying in this way, we calm our mind, heal our body, save our relationships, and help the world. We become the prayer we pray.

Metaphysical disciplines require mental boldness and a

fearless and passionate spirituality. Significant suffering and dissatisfaction with the alternatives help the spiritual flame to ignite and continue to burn. The backward drag in the early stages of one's commitment can be large. Intensity of commitment ensures that the kindling elements of devotion and dedication overcome the immense resistance to forward movement.

Spiritual Teachers

Genuine teachers tend to have, in true Zen master style, high expectations of their students. Teachers, worth their salt, take the responsibility of their students very seriously. They do not want to be held responsible for failing to set their standards high enough. As one evolves, one loses concern for being liked. One's concern, as a teacher, is the evolution of the student. Given that human nature is intrinsically and unavoidably selfish, lazy, proud, and has a great proclivity for procrastination, there are endless opportunities to confront this ego-nature in the evolving soul.

It is this approach of, sometimes, tough love combined with the sweetness of kind and gentle caring which endears our teachers to us. It also engenders an unshakeable sense of respect towards the teacher from those around. When such an individual enters the room, all those in the room lift. When such a one speaks, people listen. When such a one says *no*, it is not questioned unless there is a pressing reason to do so. When such a one is around, everyone feels better and acts better. When such a one is temporarily gone, it is a struggle to keep energy at the same level. The humanness creeps in. Sometimes, it barges in.

Who Chooses Who?

One does not really choose one's teachers. Nor do teachers choose their students. Such things are written in the heavens. It is more a matter of recognising one's teacher. Likewise, one recognises one's own students. This recognition is neither intellectual nor emotional, although intelligence, reason, and emotional resonance do play a part. It is something beyond that. It is a knowing rather than a decision. One feels a timeless connection which has become apparent and clear. One gladly surrenders to being given one's guide and advocate. Such things are destined and one is, certainly, very grateful for these precious gifts. To be such a help to another person is to repay the karma of having once been taught oneself. That is the price. We pay with love for the love we have been given.

Energetic Attraction

Of all the religions and spiritual groups in the world, why do we end up in one or, sometimes, a few? With all the people in the world, why do we closely bond with a relative few? It is destiny, karma. It is internally driven by the need for lessons and the working out of karma from past forgotten associations, agreements prior to being born, and that which will give us specific learning opportunities. Some bonds arise and then release, and some bonds remain intact. Sometimes, we cannot tell whether something is beneficial long-term. So, we let time and the flow of events decide for us. There is nothing to prove. We submit to the divine process – not another and not our own ego. It is true humility and makes us invulnerable to domination by any other human.

Fear cannot capture us, criticism cannot harm us, and pride cannot make us fall.

The Design of the Patchwork

We will frequently find that a commitment to a certain spiritual teacher will coincide with other personal relationship commitments in our life. It is as if the whole complex and intricate fabric of our lives is sewn together in an invisible pattern. Often, in retrospect, we see the design of the patchwork which, at the time, seemed unrelated or haphazard. With a little distance, the purpose and balanced nature of the pieces make perfect sense.

Energetic Field of the Teacher

When one commits to a spiritual teacher, one automatically benefits from the energetic field of that teacher. All one has to do is to sincerely say to oneself that one is a student of a certain person and it is so. One is then entitled to that teacher's energetic field. Likewise, if one wishes to extricate oneself from a particular teacher, all one has to do is to sincerely say so to oneself and it is so. The energetic bond is then broken. It does not matter if the teacher is living or deceased. It does not matter if one physically sees the teacher or not. Such things are invisible, beyond space and time, and are nonmaterial.

Alignment or Misalignment

Aligning with a spiritual teacher has serious implications. If one is drawn to an ethical, unselfish, mature, and dedicated teacher then rapid progress can be made by virtue of the field of that teacher. However, if one realises that the teacher has serious flaws or is no longer right for us then it is wise to cut the ties with that teacher. It is best to find teachers who are appropriate for our level and with whom there is an intuitive bond. Not only is one affected by the auric field of one's teacher but one will also share the karma the teacher carries. In fact, one should be very careful about proclaiming one's allegiance to any teacher or group for this reason. Such an allegiance means that you, in part, share the karma of that individual or group both good and bad. For example, in sharing a Catholic heritage, one automatically takes on board the magnificent spiritual power of all the beautiful Catholic saints, mystics, and humanitarians, as well as the very regrettable deceptions, rigidities, tyrannies, tragedies, and pain.

Dedication to Truth Not Personality

The motive of the ego is always self-centred. The love of less-developed teachers is not as unselfish as it may, sometimes, seem. Teachers can love our dedication to *them* rather than our dedication to the Truth. We dedicate ourselves to Truth, not to a material personality. We learn to lean on the sustaining Infinite and, in this way, we trust not human persons but we trust the goodness of the Divine presence. A true teacher will encourage this. The spirit of the teacher is everything. Words are cheap. Many teachers who have large followings are internally misaligned.

God-Confirmatory Not Self-Confirmatory

Success and power are very seductive elements for less-evolved spiritual teachers. A true teacher has no desire to control, needs nothing back, and will be God-confirmatory rather than self-confirmatory. Instead of seeking personal success and power, he or she will view their role as a sacred responsibility to those in need of spiritual help. For such a teacher, the joy of success is in the growth and development of others and in the fulfilment of one's own inherent gifts and destiny. To follow one's path and use one's talents is to rightly fulfil one's purpose on Earth.

Transformation

Most spiritual teachers do not consciously and intentionally deceive. However, ignorance of the ego does not make a saint. Good questions to ask about spiritual teachers are:

- Are there rules and regulations?
- Does the teacher need or want certain things back?
- Is the teacher asking for a lot of money?
- Does this teacher's presence or writing transform me?
- Do I feel closer to God by listening to this teacher?

We want the attention to be drawn not to the personal teacher but to the impersonal divinity of those listening. The focus is not on the teacher but on the true spirit within each of us. We want to feel God rising within. Otherwise, the capacity of the teacher to aid our long-term transformation will be limited. Genuine teachers quickly divert attention away from themselves. They do this so that the focus is on the needs of the student and not on themselves. If they have outgrown the desire for personal attention, they will do this very naturally. Sometimes, however, a teacher recognises a lack of gratitude in a student, in which case, he or she may deliberately and repeatedly insist on a student's profession of loyalty. It is the Zen master's stick.

Breaking the Ties

Many people instinctively wish to make breaks with certain teachers and groups in an official manner so that the bond is properly broken and the person is then freed from the invisible ties. Some people are not happy in their spiritual home but stay out of fear, laziness or ignorance. Some people clearly see the problems but stay out of love, loyalty, and duty. Spiritual freedom is a primary and essential component of a true teacher and a true group. We lose nothing by removing ourselves from a situation which is not for our highest good even if, at one stage, it was. Freedom is a non-negotiable component of spiritual love. We have our unconditional freedom to explore and go wherever is most helpful to us, whenever we feel so inspired, and to do whatever we consider to be in the highest interest of our growth and destiny.

The world is a wonderful place, full of opportunity. In this way, not only can we never be contained or destroyed but we also have complete freedom to stay, unreservedly and wholeheartedly, wherever we wish to stay and grow and help. There is no guilty, fearful or resigned staying. Rather, it is a sincere embracing of one's right place and destiny, whatever that may be. Our devotion to all that is good and all that is good for *us* becomes unshakeable. The soul's path is secure and assured. We can walk with profound peace and confidence in our hearts.

Students can be seriously let down by their teachers. It

hurts when someone we really trust disappoints us, even if it is only in our own minds. However, it gives us the opportunity to trust something better or to mature in our understanding of life, and that makes it worthwhile. Movement and change is a natural and healthy part of the path. A group or teacher may not be what we thought or we may have outgrown that particular teaching situation. We don't have to keep carrying our disappointment about moving on. We work through things as best we can and then we surrender it as soon as possible. Sometimes, we just need a change for things to settle into us and become our own. When it is a significant loss of attachment and a big disappointment, it can take a considerable time to truly get over it. We are kind to ourselves and keep working on releasing it.

Choosing Our Battles

In releasing oneself from a strong teacher or group attachment, it may be important to bravely and clearly state our disconnection. Out of respect for other's growth or out of a karmic duty we may wish to explain why we are leaving. It may be important for our development to demonstrate courage and clarity of thought. If we get upset doing so, it is understandable. We keep working on it until the emotion is released. Explaining ourselves may create more trouble than anything else, in which case, it is wisest and kindest to say nothing and quietly depart, perhaps, with a believable excuse. We do not want to hurt people unnecessarily. We may decide not to show up or correspond anymore. Certainly, most people in a group will not want to know why we are leaving them. In order to protect their own *right* position, they will simply reject us and find fault with what we say. After all, they are staying and want to feel that they are right to do so. One has to use one's energy wisely and choose one's battles. When a thing is really released within us, we do not care what others think about our departure. We are glad of our freedom and wish others the same liberty.

God is Sufficient

When one truly has God, one has no personal need for religion or spiritual groups. God is more than sufficient. However, we may still choose to remain in a religious or spiritual group. We may stay out of love. We may find that the essence of the group is beautiful, and those who are drawn to it are good. Or we may feel that the once beautiful garden of the group has become overgrown with thorny bushes, and we may wish to stay and make it a more pleasant and trouble-free place for its occupants and visitors.

Leaving the Nest

Even with the best of teachers, there is within the student an element of maintaining or reclaiming, whichever the case may be, one's spiritual independence and power. One cannot forever reside under the wings of the great protector. One is, not infrequently, pushed or pulled to venture out and strengthen one's own wings like children leaving the nest. This can all happen with good grace. There is a somewhat sad but resigned knowing that it is time. However, the form of departing is not always so conciliatory. It can be a breakdown of trust which forces the student to venture into new terrain. After enough years have passed, the old teacher is often seen with renewed affection, albeit, always in a different way.

Our First Spiritual Teacher

A combination of the stage of life, age, the particular approach to the spiritual path, the level of suffering, the developmental stage of the soul, and the personality of the departing student will influence the surrounding circumstances. *Falling in love* (in the broadest sense) with the teacher will frequently mean that the student will wholeheartedly throw him or herself into the comfort and security of the work and world of the teacher. Spiritual students with intense, enquiring, and radically-committed natures will not only devote themselves with utter abandon to the teacher but, when that nature is combined with the driving pain of human existence, such students will often tolerate little in the way of deviation from his or her expectations. One forgives such intensities when human nature is understood.

Our first serious spiritual teacher is very important to us. We tend to adore them. We, sometimes, blame them. In the end, they were the one. The first one. Many people after a first serious relationship are hurt deeply and take considerable time to heal. Future relationships are never approached in quite the same way. Hopefully, there is more independence, more forgiveness, and more wisdom about what relationships can and can't do. Any future falling apart of relationships will be handled with less pain, quicker recovery time, and more ability to accept the ups and downs of life. The same is true of spiritual teachers. Such things evolve as they should.

One Grand Brotherhood

If it is a spiritual journey, a journey drawing closer to God as we see it then the true power of the teacher is spiritual inspiration. It is the opening of Heaven's doors. It is invisible and one knows not from whence it comes and so we say it is the Spirit of God. Some call it something else. It is good and the person is loved for their contribution to others' lives. The terrain, as a spiritual student, is large and varied, continuously changing and expanding. One must follow one's inner guidance about the worth and capability of the teacher while, at the same time, remaining conscious of the limitations of teachers and the pitfalls of spiritual groups. It is one grand brotherhood of learning. One way or another, we are all in this together. Not only are the connections forged with other spiritual students but, more far-reaching, we have irrevocable bonds with all of our brothers and sisters who share Earth and who are, by nature of existence, part of the human family. If one suffers, we all suffer. What blesses one, blesses all.

Quotes

Every act of kindness, consideration, forgiveness, or love affects everyone.

— David Hawkins

It is not just spiritual truth but the degree of one's devotion to it that empowers it to become trans-formative.

— David Hawkins

There is absolutely nothing in ordinary human experience to compare with the joy of the Presence of the Love of God. No sacrifice is too great, nor effort too much, in order to realize that Presence.

— David Hawkins

It is best to choose by intuition and attraction a spiritual teacher and teachings or a school to which one feels aligned.

— David Hawkins

To strive to know God is in itself pristine and the ultimate aspiration.

— David Hawkins

The mind and all sense of a personal self disappeared. In a stunning moment, it had been replaced by an infinite, all-encompassing awareness which was radiant, complete, total, silent and still as the promised essence of All That Is. The exquisite splendour, beauty, and peace of Divinity shone forth.

— David Hawkins

Spare me the political events and power struggles, as the whole earth is my homeland and all men are my fellow countrymen.

— Kahlil Gibran

Life is a series of natural and spontaneous changes. Don't resist them; that only creates sorrow. Let reality be reality. Let things flow naturally forward in whatever way they like.

— Lao Tzu

Every step is on the path.

— Lao Tzu

I loved him as we always love for the first time; with idolatry and wild passion.

— Voltaire

The rich in spirit help the poor in one grand brotherhood, all having the same Principle, or Father.

— Mary Baker Eddy

God is our Life, and there is no other Life but that One – and that Life is perfect always.

— Thomas Hora

That they all may be one; as thou, Father, art in me, and I in thee.

— The Bible

Wisdom begins in wonder.

— Socrates

Everything on the level of personal mind is a mockery of the Divine Mind because the Divine is nondual. In Divine Reality there is no good and evil; there is only Good.

— Thomas Hora

There is no life, truth, intelligence, nor substance in matter. All is infinite Mind and its infinite manifestation, for God is All-in-all. Spirit is immortal Truth; matter is mortal error. Spirit is the real and eternal; matter is the unreal and temporal. Spirit is God, and man is His image and likeness. Therefore, man is not material; he is spiritual.

— Mary Baker Eddy

Chapter 2

The Sweetness of Love
Moving from Complete to Complete

Scale of Consciousness

Everything in the universe radiates a specific type of energy field. Dr Hawkins devised a *Scale of Consciousness* which is representative of these energy fields. Everything at the lower end of the scale has a negative, downward pulling tendency and is, essentially, harmful. The lower levels are: shame, guilt, apathy, grief, fear, desire, anger, and pride. As one moves up the scale, one enters energy fields which are increasingly life-enhancing and truth-oriented: courage, neutrality, willingness, acceptance, reason, love, and unconditional love.

Energy Field of Love

An important change occurs as the individual moves into the energy field of love. The person becomes an authentically caring and unselfish being. For all the religion, spirituality, humanitarian effort, and philosophical interest in the world, the actual presence of someone at a truly loving level of consciousness is not a common experience. Love and devotion are soul mates. Love is devotion and devotion is love. The quality of spiritual devotion is recognisable by the presence of goodness, beauty, harmony, and inner confidence. Compassion becomes a marked quality of presence. Such individuals have a look of serenity and peacefulness. They automatically send healing light into the world.

The height of this level is inhabited by gifted healers, saints, and spiritual leaders. It is also the domain of those who choose to remain in the world in such a way that other people do not recognise their greatness. They quietly and undetected continue their mission, purposely indistinguishable to the average person. They are known to God as bringers of light but unknown and unrecognised by most of humanity. The presence of someone at a loving level of consciousness is innately uplifting. Even the entry point of this level carries an enormous amount of spiritual power. People are instinctively drawn to such an individual and feel better around him or her. The nature of such a one is delightful and irresistible but, also, powerful. Do not underestimate the power of this level of consciousness. One with God, at this level, is a majority over opposing forces.

Glowing

How sweetly one glows when one is imbued with love. Some time ago, I attended a talk given by a swami. A swami is the equivalent of a monk or nun, one who has renounced ordinary social life for the dedicated following of a religious path or teacher. I instantly liked her. She radiated calmness, intelligence, and kindness. Her talk was on love and sweetness. One of the endearing things she said was that when we have developed our capacity to love, we will not need to wear perfume because the body will have a beautiful, sweet smell. Love is demonstrated by our undivided attention and genuine interest in another's well-being. The loving individual has the capacity to look people in the eye with quiet confidence and sincere concern. Whenever we move into a loving space, we lift our consciousness and become a beacon of light. Our aim is to be that consistently – a truly healing presence.

An interesting response to someone who authentically loves is tears. It is a grateful, relieved, emotional reaction to being in a situation of safety and trust. Tears are a natural response to being in a healing environment. Our psyche grabs the opportunity to release built up stress, emotional charge, and damage. Tears help to heal internal, energetic scarring from all the myriad of pains one suffers from life, karma, and evolution. The soul feels relief from being uplifted, rescued, and encouraged. Tears are also an alignment with spiritual clarity, purity, and integrity. There is a feeling of being at home. We have an instinctive, deep response to goodness, beauty, and enduring love.

Willingness

Part of love is willingness. Willingness to serve others and generosity of spirit are returned to us as generosity from life. Money, happiness, friendships, purpose, and freedom from suffering are some of the rewards. Even if we had all the money and free time in the world which is the ultimate goal of many people, there is, nevertheless, an intrinsic need in humankind to serve a higher purpose and to love. One of the most frequent illnesses of middle-aged, professional people is depression stemming from an achievement of their financial and professional goals and a consequent emptiness. To offer what we are capable of offering will transform our life. Wherever we are, whatever we understand, whatever level of consciousness we are living from, we can willingly give. And, of course, the essence of giving is the desire to love.

Real love is not just soft. It is, also, strong. To be loving does not equate with being nice. Sometimes, to be nice is loving. Sometimes, to be nice is not what is needed. Niceness can be ineffectual weakness. It is not love to condone mediocrity or to allow destructiveness. It would not be loving to allow someone to hurt our child. It would not be loving to allow our friend to go down a destructive path without being honest with them. It would not be loving to ourselves to accept abuse, harm or negativity. We stand steadfastly for the protection of our own being. We also take very seriously the guardianship of those in our care.

Nice is Not Always Nice

Being nice may *seem* loving but it can be driven by a diverse range of underlying motives such as wanting to be liked, fear of rejection or wanting a favour. All of these motives are weak and inherently do not work. Trying to be popular never gets the result. Trying to be loved never makes us loved. Trying to get respect never makes us respected. Pacifying and being conciliatory towards damaging people does not turn them into well-intended, trustworthy creatures.

Intention is everything. Is there love in what a person says or is there underlying ill-will in their words? Intention will determine the destined outcome of any situation. The same kind words from one person can be a healing balm and from another person, a sweet poison. The same harsh words from one person can be malice and from another person, save a life. The intention behind the action or thought is always what makes it weak or strong, effective or ineffective, healing or powerless.

To be truly loving and kind means to honestly and genuinely have the highest good of the person at heart. This can manifest as soft or confrontational. It depends on what is being dealt with at the time. In the end, anything which carries the power of true, unselfish, and courageous love will have the power to protect, heal, and transform. Everything else is fraught with problems. The way that a spiritually-oriented person offers love may not always be conventional. He or she may say things that other people do not understand. They may, sometimes, seem strange or harsh. They may, other times, seem very soft and kind when other people do not think it is appropriate. People can find such a person unpredictable and even illogical. A spiritually-directed person sees so much more than other people. He or she sees the intentions behind other people's words and actions and responds to that. Generally, others cannot see the same thing and so they can neither understand nor predict the actions of the developed soul. There is a certain respect and, sometimes, nervousness which develops as a result.

Contentment

A self-contained person has no need for idle conversation. Idle conversation is the fabric and hallmark of socialising. Others may not understand one's lack of enthusiasm about engaging in socially acceptable but, generally, trivial conversations, dinners, get-togethers, and outings. However, when the situation calls for it, such a person can be the master of human convention and conversation. One of the attributes of Abraham Maslow's self-actualised person is that while capable of creating excellent quality relationships, he or she will often choose a small group of a trusted few.

In terms of happiness, the great requirement is fulfilment of our own destiny, to do our best with what we have, and to meet the challenges we are called upon to meet in this lifetime. That will bring us happiness and contentment. Add to that a growing capacity to love and accept love, and one's happiness and contentment simply magnify. It is enough to be oneself, do what we can, like what we instinctively like, learn what is within our grasp, and practice what is in our own heart. There are always many behind us and many before us. To look either way too much will only make us proud or hopeless. We are who we are. That is enough and God asks nothing more.

Family Tension

Many people think that it is only their own family that is dysfunctional and try to keep such things secret. Holiday periods, in particular, are notorious for family friction. If the tension gets strained enough, it will erupt leaving those in its wake battered and bewildered. The first step to healing such feuds and tensions is to be honest about their existence. The second is to discern the underlying issues which are beneath the, usually, trivial setting-off of the conflict. The third is to let wisdom and common sense speak about either boundary setting or, if it is possible, an honest and sincere reconciliation. Fourth, regardless of one's decisions and actions, without forgiveness we will accumulate yet another grudge, adding to the many that are already part of a normal human consciousness. To carry a grudge is to shorten one's life, poison one's health, and contract one's heart. Knowing this makes forgiveness an easier choice.

In many cases, under the guise of righteousness or entitlement or supposed care for another's well-being, people will seek their own perceived victory. It may be driven by the desire for money, power seeking or jealousy. Silent but poisonous jealousy compares itself to another, comes out worse, and then seeks to undermine the other in order to make itself feel better about its own mistakes and shortcomings. Of course, in most people, all this is entirely unconscious and rarely acknowledged. They are ugly qualities and few will face and seek to eliminate them. What seems sweet to the ego is poison to the fulfilment of one's soul and to true happiness. If people knew this, they would not be so tempted to betray that which is truly good for short-term gains which have the smell of sickness and duplicity.

Good Grace

In the end, in spite of ugly human traits, we must forgive it all, let it go, and release it from our preoccupied thoughts. After all, what is an ego to do? It is programmed for self-preservation. It sees personal gain as pivotal to its survival and success. It is only by dedicated, inward searching and the practice of embarrassing honesty with ourselves that we see these qualities or the seeds of these qualities in ourselves and thereby recognise them in others. We know what jealousy feels like. We know what the desire for power looks like. We know the prickly touch of resentment. We know the smell of money with its seductive call to a better, less stressful, and happier life. If we are human, we know these things.

If we are fortunate enough to be on a mental and spiritual path which clearly recognises these human foibles, we will gradually correct them. They will be replaced with a more mature, sincere, and loving approach to life. Surely, then, we can have the good grace to understand that those who are not yet on that path, do not have the ability to make the choices which are obvious to us from where we are standing. In the valley, some things which seemed like a great choice or even the only choice, look ridiculous from higher up the mountain path. Pain is the fuel of growth and each must suffer from unwise choices until the consciousness has matured enough to choose otherwise. Let us not be too hasty to damn those who do not yet have the good fortune of being on a path which leads to peace, success, and safety. The price of that path is willingness to share it with others and willingness to forgive those who do not yet know it is there.

Taking the Lead

It is best for the more spiritually advanced person in a relationship to take the lead in areas which require spiritual wisdom. In this way, both people will benefit and be free to continue their development unfettered. Many pitfalls will be avoided. If the lesser evolved person takes the lead then the other person will become frustrated in his or her being. The lesser evolved person will also have a tendency to remain at the level they feel comfortable with. To be spiritually more evolved is not synonymous with calling oneself spiritual. Many so-called spiritual people radiate superiority. Contrary to having a genuinely superior nature their lives are full of problems, relationship breakdowns, illness, and financial incompetence. Personal weaknesses such as pride, anger, emotional immaturity, jealousy, and denial about the state of one's own being are frequently over-looked. Self-righteousness, moral superiority, and desire for control do not belong in the realm of the spiritually trustworthy.

The true spiritual student is humble, gracious, patient, kind, wise, brave, protective, direct, and intelligent. He or she seeks the good of God above all else. He or she has a deep understanding of human nature which comes from much time looking into one's own thoughts. Seeking attention and approval will have been outgrown. There will be an emotional and spiritual independence. The combination of love, compassion, wisdom, and courage makes such an individual safe to follow. Whichever of the two people more closely resembles this then it is best for that person to take the lead in areas which need that type of wisdom. Taking the lead, far from putting one in a position of personal advantage, means to take on the sacred responsibility to protect the soul of the other person. This is in addition to one's automatic responsibility to care for oneself.

Spoiling

Spoiling someone is not love. It creates misery for those who live the illusion that life rotates around them, that they are entitled. Spoiling loved ones is not an endearing quality of loving. It is a disservice to oneself and the loved one. This also applies to dogs. We may believe that we are unselfishly caring for our loved ones by putting their needs and desires before our own but, actually, we may simply be spoiling them. Love does what is truly best for the others' long-term development and happiness. Spoiling someone is driven by insecurity – a desire to be liked, loved, approved of, and accepted. True love is driven by wisdom, self-confidence, unselfishness, and common sense. It seeks to encourage the growth of independence in the other so that true self-respect can germinate.

It is a mistake to dishonour our own happiness in favour of another. There is a certain type of person – good and self-sacrificing but lacking in self-worth – who can, and frequently does, make this mistake to their great personal detriment. They have been mentally programmed to value others above themselves and so will put the needs and desires of others first in the belief that it is the right and caring thing to do. To put others' needs before our own and to disregard our own needs is to misunderstand what love is and how life works. Out of loyalty to a relative, friend or colleague, we may dishonour our own destiny because we feel uncomfortable about claiming what is ours. Not only will we destroy our future happiness and destiny but the other person will, almost inevitably, not appreciate the sacrifice we have made. They can easily become the ungrateful brat or the precious princess. Or, at least, they may take on that persona in their relationship with us.

Our Primary Responsibility

We include ourselves in the right for happiness as an equally worthy recipient of good. Not only do we include ourselves but our first responsibility is to our own well-being because that is the life that God has given us to care for. However, we do so with the balance of knowing that part of caring for ourselves is caring for others. It is certainly true that the greater one's capacity to honour one's own being with truth, passion, dedication, and respect then the greater is one's capacity to honour the nature of all other beings.

The higher form of love is to understand that we are all one, that our own good is equal to and part of another's good. It is an understanding of the higher spiritual principles. What is good for one is good for all. What blesses one, blesses all. If one suffers, we all suffer. If one awakens spiritually, it will radiate out into the entire world. In this way, to follow one's own path of happiness is neither selfish nor unselfish. It is the natural way to harmonise with the life principle of *good attracts good*.

Relationship Status

In life, there are so many people who need love but we cannot personally love everyone. We must find those who belong to our own particular karmic groupings. How do we make such important decisions? Whenever we decide to invest a considerable amount of time in one person or a group of people, we can make that choice based on a feeling of rightness in our soul. The rightness may be recognisable by a sense of peace or happiness or balance. It may be recognisable by a sense of destiny unfolding as it should. It could be that the thought of leaving someone or something, in some form, feels distinctly unsatisfactory. Many of our human connections are not logically explainable. They come from the unconscious. The unconscious, karma, and destiny are all siblings. Karmic connectedness means that we are destined to play a part in certain people's lives because we have a higher connection which cannot be easily broken.

A mature person feels complete in all stages of life and personal relationship status. The soul is happy single, as well as in a relationship. It is a mistake to think that we need a certain type of relationship to be happy. If we crave a relationship when we are single, we will bring that wanting into any relationship with the consequent problems. To feel that destiny will provide us with what best meets our deepest needs is to be able to enter into any stage of life with confidence and a sense of completeness, not a sense of lack which someone else is supposed to fill.

Transitions

Relationship transitions are an inevitable part of human life, in one form or another. However, in the grand scheme of things they are nothing to be concerned about. Souls come and go, in various ways, in and out of our life over great eons of time. We never lose someone we love. The bond is eternal. As relationships transform, the door is opened to new developments which are very important for our spiritual progress. Nothing is lost. When we are on the spiritual path, everything is a gain. Every stage of life is perfect when we look for the genuine blessing in it. By practicing to be loving, not only do we become more loving but we also find that much love is returned to us. We find love by being loving. We need not ever feel alone, afraid or rejected because love is, indeed, everywhere around us. A confident and fearless attitude to life and a knowledge that we will always be taken care of, allows us to extend a generosity of spirit to all our dear ones.

Intimacy

In order to enjoy a close and intimate bond with our partner, we need to be mindful of the emotional state of the relationship. Without an honest and genuine emotional bond of trust, a high-quality sexual relationship will never be achieved. Sex will become non-existent or the domain of one controlling partner over one submissive partner or a mutual using of each other person's body. Each individual brings with them all that they are outside the bedroom walls into the sanctity of the enclosed bedroom space. With humour, goodwill, and enthusiasm the skill level of both people can improve rapidly. A few good sex books can do wonders for a couple. We cannot assume that our partner understands the sexual needs of a body that has a different physical and emotional functioning to our own. Even gay couples cannot assume to know how a different person functions sexually, though it is the same structural type of body. Every good-natured experiment is one step closer to a more satisfying experience. A couple may even choose to investigate such ideas as the meridians and pressure points of Taoist foreplay if they would like their sexual relationship to become more holistic and healing.

Currents of the Sea

An individual's sexual energy level can alter dramatically with illness and tensions, well-being and happiness, alternate interests, and the ongoing cycles of life. The ebb and flow of sexual interest is as changeable and, sometimes, unpredictable as the currents of the sea. Like everything else in life, spiritual students respond to sexual matters through the eyes of love and wisdom. It is no secret that men are usually more driven by sex than women. However, this can vary over the years with stress, age, personality, the state of the relationship, and other issues. Communication and a desire to make the relationship work are important. Compromise is a good path if it helps another and does not harm us. If one person feels that they need more sex than the other, a regular and mutually agreed quota is sometimes enough to fix the problem. The one needing more sex will find the patience to wait. The other will relax, knowing that they will not be consistently harassed and they will put their energy into making the night special.

A quota may not seem very romantic but the reality of sex is, often, far from romantic. It is, frequently, the stewing pot of friction. It is so fragile that the smallest things can sabotage the whole event. For most people, it has innumerable problems. Yet, in spite of this, it has a naked, mystical essence that relentlessly and, almost, ruthlessly draws together those souls that have a secret to share with each other. While the romantic looks a little soppy and self-absorbed to me, the true lover has a healthy, robust, earthy, strong, and loving attractor field which automatically asks for a like response in his or her partner. Do not underestimate the capacity of your partner to grow through the intimacy of sexual union. Both men and women need to be strong, confident, forthright, kind, gentle, and nurturing. In the bedroom, three are present – the partners and the Divine. Use the openness and vulnerability of the sexual arena to grow closer to God and give that same gift to your loved one.

Attractiveness as an Energy Field

One of the quickest ways to destroy a sexual relationship is neediness. Without doubt, neediness in sex will rebound into some form of rejection. What a paradox – the thing that is desired must be released in order to be gained. The more we want it, the less we will have it. Some men and women seem to have mastered the genuine, non-needy approach to sex. Independence is a highly attractive quality.

It may not be the highest human quality but, rest assured, without independence and lack of neediness the individual will not be able to progress past a certain point on the emotional and spiritual path.

There is a direct correlation between the level of neediness and the level of attractiveness, regardless of age and physical appearance. As we become emotionally and spiritually independent, we automatically radiate a stronger auric field. This is interpreted as attractiveness by other people. Fortunately, as we progress, we have less desire to use individual qualities such as attractiveness as a means of controlling others for personal gain. The person who is desired must learn to love others in a way which is helpful and kind but without taking advantage of the interest other people have in them. Many fallen-gurus have fallen because of this seduction. The lure of using personal attractiveness for selfish gain is significant. However, to do so means an instant fall from grace in the Divine hierarchy. Part of the responsibility of spiritual power is to not use it selfishly. Of course, people make mistakes with this issue but no mistake is permanent if the error is seen and sincerely corrected.

Transforming Sexual Energy

At various times in our life, we may wish to transform sexual energy into higher energy which is useful for spiritual development. This can happen spontaneously and unconsciously such as when it is not possible to discharge sexual energy in a normal, healthy sexual relationship. It can, sometimes, happen that those in the process of intensive, creative work will temporarily cease sexual activity in order to channel all of their energy into their work. Top level athletes will often refrain from sexual activity before an important event in order to save their life-force for the task at hand. The lack of a suitable mate can trigger the automatic transfer of frustrated sexual energy into the higher energy centres where it will be used for the mental, creative, and spiritual progress of that individual.

To an extent, transforming sexual energy is an inbuilt and independent function of our being. Some physical activities can have the tendency to transfer sexual energy just by our participation in them. Physical activities which have a parallel higher purpose are most conducive to this process. Thoughtful contemplation and peaceful awareness can be practiced while walking. Harmony of body, mind, and spirit is engendered in yoga. A sincere, heartfelt connection is foundational to beautiful dancing, music, and art. It encourages the heart to focus on love and things invisible. It invites the soul to listen to the silent music of the interwoven notes of human existence. Challenging mental work or any work done in the right spirit, including housework and gardening, can have the same effect. In fact, those in the habit of continuous prayer know that everything is an opportunity for communion with God and inner consciousness work.

Rising Life-Force

For many thousands of years, Eastern spiritual traditions have spoken of the life-force of the body as running up the spine through the energy centres and through the etheric body. The etheric body, auric field or energy around a person has the imprint of all that occurs at the physical level of that person's unique body and experiences. It is possible and, at times, desirable to aid the movement of the life-force upwards to higher planes. The base level energy is visualised as moving upwards in the body and auric field. Such a practice is possible when one has healthy, strong, and positive energy at the lower energy centres. If one is depressed, unwell, unhealthy or lethargic then there will be no available energy to move to the higher energy centres.

At a basic, primitive level of functioning, mankind's sexual behaviour is both unconscious and only minimally controlled. It is driven by natural instinct and controlled only by whatever social conventions the individual accepts as mandatory. The drive is fuelled by the desire to release pent-up sexual energy which, if not released, feels unpleasant. Love is neither desired nor sought. Even liking the mate is not a high priority. At this level, suitable partners are, at least theoretically, innumerable because the requirements are so low. As the individual develops, he or she develops the desire for a more suitable mate, with more compatible qualities. The person's own qualities, by this stage, have considerably developed and so they are capable of attracting a higher-level mate into their life.

Servants of God

However, if the individual continues to mature to an unusually high level of development, they will find that the availability of suitable mates reduces dramatically as the requirements of the person become more and more sophisticated and specialised. In fact, at this level of consciousness, the person relies heavily on Universal guidance to find the right partner as so few individuals are actually suitable. In the meantime, however, they will use the opportunity of, perhaps, long periods of sexual abstinence to channel the energy into spiritual growth and so no loss is overly felt, if it is felt at all.

For some advanced spiritual beings, the sexual life-force seems to remain dormant. Its potential is not realised in an active form but is retained within the individual adding to the energetic power of the individual. It is consciously used for other purposes. Above those who use their energy for creative and intellectual pursuits are those few advanced beings whose very presence on Earth balances and heals the calibration of Earth's energy field. They bless us with their presence and protect, what is still, a primitive planet from further self-harm until such time as we seek healing, health, and harmony as a collective totality.

Quotes

In the higher levels of consciousness, life moves from complete to complete.

— David Hawkins

People say they can't find love as though it were something to be gotten. Once one becomes willing to give love, the discovery quickly follows that one is surrounded by love and merely didn't know how to access it. Love is actually present everywhere and its presence only needs to be realized.

— David Hawkins

Be kind to everything and everyone, including oneself, all the time, with no exception.

— David Hawkins

Love is benign, supportive, and nurtures life; consequently, it is the level of true happiness...It is discovered that Love is available everywhere and that lovingness results in the return of love.

— David Hawkins

Lovingness is a way of relating to the world. It is a generosity of attitude that expresses itself in seemingly small but powerful ways. It is a wish to bring happiness to others, to brighten their day and lighten their load.

— David Hawkins

Let no one ever come to you without leaving better and happier. Be the living expression of God's kindness: kindness in your face, kindness in your eyes, kindness in your smile.

— Mother Teresa

Criticism may not be agreeable, but it is necessary. It fulfils the same function as pain in the human body. It calls attention to an unhealthy state of things.

— Winston Churchill

Being deeply loved by someone gives you strength, while loving someone deeply gives you courage.

— Lao Tzu

Take no thought for what should be or what should not be; seek ye first to know the good of God, which already is. (Second Principle of Metapsychiatry)

— Thomas Hora

Behold my mother and my brethren! For whosoever shall do the will of my Father which is in heaven, the same is my brother, and sister, and mother.

— The Bible

Blessed are the shouldless for their lives will be fussless.

— Thomas Hora

When making a decision of minor importance, I have always found it advantageous to consider all the pros and cons. In vital matters, however, such as the choice of a mate or a profession, the decision should come from the unconscious, from some-where within ourselves. In the important decisions of personal life, we should be governed, I think, by the deep inner needs of our nature.

— Sigmund Freud

We choose our joys and sorrows long before we experience them.

— Kahlil Gibran

The behaviour of a human being in sexual matters is often a prototype for the whole of his other modes of reaction in life.

— Sigmund Freud

A woman should soften but not weaken a man.

— Sigmund Freud

Because one believes in oneself, one doesn't try to convince others. Because one is content with oneself, one doesn't need others' approval. Because one accepts oneself, the whole world accepts him or her.

— Lao Tzu

Chapter 3

Grist for the Mill
Working Through Issues

Student

Everyone is a "spiritual student" doing "spiritual work" because everyone is here and has to cope, one way or another, with life. The difference is that an aware person learns from their pain and they eventually create a happy life. An unaware person also has pain. However, as they do not know (or do not want to know) how to help themselves, they learn little or nothing from their pain. Thus, their journey to happiness is long and indirect. The process of change includes going into our painful emotions rather than running away from them or attempting to kill them with drugs or alcohol or any other means of temporary pain relief.

Spiritual Work

Many people wait until a crisis before they are willing to question their way of being in the world. However, as spiritual students, we have constant work in the moment-by-moment content of daily human life. We consistently practice the principles of healing and consciousness evolution. In many cases, this will prevent acute problems and crises from occurring. When they do occur, the healing process is already very familiar and so the stage of suffering is greatly reduced and, sometimes, completely eliminated. We can thus use all experiences of pain as grist for the mill of our spiritual development.

Upsetting experiences tend to connect us with the underlying energy field which lies beneath our awareness. Some of its accumulated pressure is released. When we are distressed, we enter the lower energy fields of fear, anger, guilt, pride, apathy, grief, shame, and hatred. As we become connected to one of these negative fields, the others tend to join force. We often start to remember numerous buried, corresponding experiences and memories. They have been triggered in our mind and will bring up the linked emotions. All are opportunities that are asking to be healed. As someone once said to me, "When the negative emotions start pouring out, it feels as if I have to heal the whole world from its very beginning."

This is the place where the real spiritual work is happening. Reading, studying, and thinking are merely preparation for the real work of authentic, deep, internal transformation. Without the latter, we are just playing around; amusing our egotistic, mental selfhood. Real spiritual work can be tough and, at some places, very tough but it is worth it for what it brings. After a while, the new light brings such a fresh easiness that one forgets the toughness. Sometimes, one can even feel that it has always been a bright, breezy, and beautiful walk in the park, although some places may have been a very dark wood.

Crises and Resistance

Healing is initially aided by surrendering to whatever has happened. We accept that it has, in fact, happened. We do not deny it. We do not fight it. We do not run away and hide. Denial, resistance, and running away are great barriers to healing and will only exacerbate the suffering. The mind tries to use reason to manage crises and suffering. However, the rational mind will be overwhelmed with the far more virulent content of the swirling energy field of fear and sadness which is released in intense suffering or a crisis.

When we become willing to go deeply into the energy field which is spontaneously activated by acute pain, we draw one step closer to our higher self. Suffering initially brings about feelings of loss and powerlessness. Strong negative emotions come rushing to the surface. These are the repressed emotions of many forgotten experiences of the soul. These emotions are also part of the collective consciousness of every group we belong to – family, race, country, humanity.

Release and Balance

We learn to go deeply into these emotions and the underlying energy field of the experience in order to see it through, ride it out, and let it come to a natural release. Balance is then brought to the psyche. The whole experience must be bravely faced with the knowledge that such an opportunity is beneficial to one's development and will have substantial rewards. The fear is temporary. The rewards are permanent.

A seemingly small incident can sometimes give rise to

emotion that seems to far outweigh the current situation. This is because each issue which arises in our life carries the emotion of the current situation and also a stack of similar situations with similar emotion. A rejection, for example, can bring great despair as if an irrational force has overtaken us. Each painful situation is an opportunity to work through and heal the stacks of repressed emotion which keep us from the goal of spiritual evolution. Bringing up unconscious memories and hidden pain may not be easy but they hold the record of our past issues. We learn from them and then we release them. In this way, we draw closer to the serene stillness and profound peace we ultimately seek.

Group Healing

The healing process can happen simultaneously to a whole group of people. An issue that has seemingly come out of nowhere can ignite in the entire group intense feelings which cover the whole gamut of emotion. The issue will have connected that group with a mass of swirling feelings which were previously unconscious and, perhaps, unconscious for a very long time. The more ferocious the force that has been unleashed, the more it clearly belongs to the karma of that group. They must own it as their own issue. It will be deep-seated, important, far-reaching, and probably mostly unconscious. Whole groups of bonded people can concurrently undergo transformational change and growth.

Repression

Major fears, sadness, and anger tend to be repressed because they are unpleasant to face. We do not know how to deal with them. Of course, society demands restraint. We obviously cannot rant and rave to every person we feel annoyed with. We cannot go around angrily blaming every poor soul that crosses our path. We cannot crumble into a bumbling heap of fear whenever we are challenged or anxious. We cannot crawl into a little ball of despair and refuse to face the world because we are disheartened and sad. Hopefully, as a child, we learned some restraint and level-headedness. However, we transfer these necessary learned responses into indiscriminate repression.

As repressions grow, they take more energy to hold down and the effort to do so robs us of our peace, ability to relate to others with honesty, and capacity to face issues calmly and rationally. In the heat of surfacing repressions which have been inadvertently unleashed, rationality is the last thing to be listened to. Exploding repressed emotion is not interested in calm rationality. It simply wants to vent. When one understands this, situations which would other-wise seem disastrous can often be viewed with wisdom, patience, and even humour. The personal ego takes itself very seriously for no good reason.

Raving Lunatics to Peaceful Warriors

We have a fear that if we go into our deeper emotions, we will be consumed by them. We fear that if we close the door of our bedroom and face the emotion then we will be consumed by the monstrous darkness of our inner being. We think our fears will turn us into a neurotic mess of blub-ber, our angers will turn us into raving lunatics, and our sadness will be so overwhelming that we will never function in the world again. It is not so. One only has to practice this a few times to know that, far from destroying us, going into our inner thoughts deeply works them through to their conclusion or, at least, to some degree of conclusion. The intensity of the emotion lifts and we are left with a far greater ability to find our peace and happiness. As we become more proficient at this process, the time it takes becomes shorter and the resulting peace and assurance becomes more substantial and unshakeable.

We can determine to not let the issue go until we have received the blessing from it. The blessing will absolutely come if we just stick in there, see it through, and don't desert our post. Our post is the watch we keep over our own thoughts. The battle is with our own consciousness which hovers between the old land and the new. The enemy is the thoughts and attached emotions which bind our soul to lower level thinking, without us even knowing where it comes from. One has to beckon the spiritual warrior inside oneself whenever it is deemed necessary for the task at hand. Courage is the fuel. Healing is the direction. Forgiveness is the balm. Love is the atmosphere Divine.

Pride

We do not have to look far to see the destructive trail of prideful people. Arrogant, delusional, self-absorbed, full of denial, and bent on the downfall of their supposed enemies; such people leave a path of debris. They lose their friends and family members, have enemies at work, find that very few people enjoy their company, attract the temporary friendship of equally angry folk, and generally suffer the consequences of physical and emotional illness and life-hardships.

The healing of pride requires self-honesty and, surprisingly, self-acceptance. Arrogant pride compensates for a deep lack of confidence and is built on an underlying shame. In that sense, arrogant pride is better than shame. It is at least capable of getting up and doing something, unlike depressive despair and shame. A genuine acceptance of one's own intrinsic worth diminishes the need to have artificial pride. One is then able to move into a more constructive energy field, where one is not always looking to claim one's superiority and fight those who do not accordingly honour one's self-inflated value. Self-acceptance is calmer and kinder. It is not antagonistic or defensive. It is amenable and obliging.

Pride Goes Before the Fall

Pride sets up its own demise by provoking counter attack from other egos. *Pride goes before the fall.* Humility, however, tends to invite the appreciation of others. Pride invites criticism and a desire to pull down the inflated ego. Those immersed in pride are highly defensive because, in their mind, they are fighting for the survival of their most precious selfhood. When one is accepting of one's many and varied limitations and the general limitations of being human, there is no need to be defensive. Short-comings are corrected and often viewed in oneself and others as the inevitable stupidity of both the personal and collective ego.

Pride is the horse drawing the cart of the ego. Both the horse and the cart are to be abandoned. Spiritual seekers have a tendency to replace normal egotistical pride with the pride of the so-called spiritual ego. Spiritual pride is taking personal ownership of spiritual gifts and healings or growth that has been achieved. The ego does not care how we rationalise its existence, so long as it derives enough power to maintain its life-force.

Reasonable pride has its place in ordinary human life, for example, one would not wish to take away the pride of a child's growing self-confidence or the temporary pride of a job well done. However, as a spiritual student it is a quality we can ill afford to cultivate. As we evolve, we become aware of the subtle and deceptive workings of pride. We learn to recognise pride as an ego-function. Pride, in its various forms, feeds the ego and keeps it thriving. As we desire to express unconditional love, compassion, and pure spiritual intention, we cannot afford the luxury of feeding the ego. The demise of the ego hastens our path.

Depression

Depression, in one form or other, is a common part of the human experience. Depression can be a helpful learning opportunity in that it is our soul's way of saying, "Something is not right here. I need to change something. I am feeling bad and that means I need to spiritually reorient myself." This, in turn, leads to a more spiritually evolved person and one who becomes increasingly less vulnerable to sadness and depression. The basis of depression is, frequently, that we have placed the source of our happiness outside ourselves. This makes us automatically vulnerable to depression, anxiety, fear, and loss. Ultimately, to feel separated from anything which is deemed essential for our happiness is to feel shut off from God. We must take back our power and refuse to be the helpless victim of some perceived loss or lack. We start to look at it differently, as a learning opportunity. This breeds confidence and hope. It is a process of healing and evolution and lessens the capacity to feel separated from anything and everything which is good.

Courage

Spiritual students, sometimes, have the misguided notion that because they try to live a loving life, they will be free of enemies. There is a belief that all situations of enmity can be healed. Such is not the case and it serves us well to realise this. These same spiritual students can end up as appeasers. Many situations can be healed by love, however, love is not appeasement. Love is based on courage and carries a great deal of power. Appeasement is weak, automatically disrespected by others, and is inherently powerless. It is the nature of human existence that those who coexist on our planet will have many points of friction.

At some level of awareness, our thoughts are not hidden from others. Most people have an uneasy feeling about someone who is jealous of them. The wise student of life understands the competitive nature of the ego and its inherent capacity for jealousy. Dr. Hawkins would tell his students, *Treat the ego like a pet.* It needs to be controlled but we must not be too harsh with its instinctive, inherited nature. Instead of being jealous, we can choose to align with those we admire and, thereby, learn from them and substantially improve our life. We can replace the tendency for jealousy which is an automatic part of the ego's make-up with appreciation of others. The troublesome life will then turn into a good life and the good life will turn into a great life.

Courage is the starting point of everything good. To love another is to automatically feed the fire of courage. Everyone knows a mother will do anything to protect her children. Love turns the gentle lamb into a lion. Love gives us a mighty weapon. We cannot be humiliated when we are fighting for someone or something we love. We will not give up when we are fighting for loved ones. We will certainly die for that which we hold dearer than our own life. Do not underestimate the power of one who loves. An enemy who fights for selfish reasons can always be defeated and will have weak spots and limitations. One who fights for love will not concede. As we evolve, those loved ones extend out from one's family to include all of humanity. We need courage to keep going, to try again, to value ourselves and our destiny. Courage is the basis of greatness. It is also the basis of all growth. No matter who we are or what we must do in life, we will need courage to progress and grow.

All Fear is Fallacious

Courage and confidence will grow over the years with practice and self-awareness. Even the weakest and most scared of us can become brave. One simply has to realise that the alternative is worse. To follow our fears, betray our soul, dishonour our talents, remain silent when a voice is required, and fail to protect those in our care is worse than anything that could happen to us by standing our ground. We are never alone. God will help us. God has all the power of Life and beyond. We learn to have confidence in Grace to save and help us so that, each day, our courage grows. Such is the courage that gains respect from others. More importantly, we gain respect for ourselves.

We do not let fear, worry, hurt or stress deter us from our course. The Divine unceasingly guides and protects us. There is nothing to be afraid of and no grounds for worry. Our greatest protection is to understand that, ultimately,

God's laws prevail. They are love, understanding, peace, health, beauty, kindness, serenity, freedom, and courage. It is not possible to be seduced by the lure of ego-gratification or intimidated by the tyranny of impostors when each one of us is as the angels. We are loved beyond comprehension. So, we must claim our rightful inheritance and live with the confidence of protection.

Quotes

The person who is involved in spiritual work is always looking at what is occurring in life, seeing it as the teacher, as the grist for the mill.

— David Hawkins

To try to escape (the pain) will only prolong it. The faster one opens it up, the faster the energy is let out, and the quicker the experience will be over.

— David Hawkins

Acute catastrophes are the times when we make great leaps. These are the golden opportunities that are priceless.

— David Hawkins

One basic truth that is of inestimable value and usefulness is the dictum that all fear is fallacious. Fear is overcome by walking directly through it until one breaks through into the joy that the fear is blocking.

— David Hawkins

Out of suffering have emerged the strongest souls; the most massive characters are seared with scars.

— Kahlil Gibran

If you meet a woman who sails her life with strength and grace and assurance, talk to her. What you will find is that there has been a suffering, that at some time she has left herself for dead.

— Carl Jung

Unexpressed emotions will never die. They are buried alive and will come forth later in uglier ways.

— Sigmund Freud

Keep me away from the wisdom which does not cry, the philosophy which does not laugh and the greatness which does not bow before children.

— Kahlil Gibran

A great man is always willing to be little.

> — Ralph Waldo Emerson

Though we travel the world over to find the beautiful, we must carry it with us, or we find it not.

> — Ralph Waldo Emerson

You have enemies? Good. That means you've stood up for something, sometime in your life.

> — Winston Churchill

An appeaser is one who feeds a crocodile—hoping it will eat him last.

> — Winston Churchill

Envy is a desire to have what someone else has. Jealousy is a desire to be what someone else is. Rivalry is a desire to be better than someone else. Malice is ill will.

> — Thomas Hora

How does envy start? By comparison thinking. Every one of us is a unique manifestation of infinite, divine Love-Intelligence, and there are no two individuals alike. Therefore, it makes no sense to compare, and if we do compare, we fail to bring into manifestation our uniqueness and to find fulfilment in life.

— Thomas Hora

If you are not afraid of dying, there is nothing you cannot achieve.

— Lao Tzu

I am under no laws but God's.

— A Course in Miracles

Give unto Caesar what is Caesar's and God what is God's.

— The Bible

Chapter 4

Healing

A Sacred Path

Living Prayer

W hen I was in my early twenties, before my time with Dr Hora, I happily belonged to a Catholic Charismatic group. I lived in two of its communal houses and embraced community life with great enthusiasm. Such Pentecostal groups view the miraculous as common and healing as the reachable result of sincere and dedicated prayer. Faith was alive. Prayer was common. Dedication was the norm. All expected their lives to improve and whole-heartedly dedicated their days to God, in much the same way as many religious orders do. As there were so many young people drawn to the community, it was also fun and full of laughter. It was, indeed, a wonderful time. I felt very fortunate to find a religious group that was alive, vibrant, and flourishing. I was able to live like a member of a religious order while being a lay person. I would say that the short-coming of such groups is the vulnerability to fundamentalist thinking and its associated problems.

Miracles

Kathleen Evans had a healing of lung and brain cancer in 1993. The events which led to the healing are in line with what one would consider ripe grounds for a natural healing. That is not to say it was not miraculous but that the miraculous would be far more commonplace if there was a greater understanding of the Divine. When the higher laws of spiritual existence are more fully comprehended, healing often becomes the inevitable and gratefully accepted consequence of aligning oneself with a more spiritual position.

After a normal life with all its ups and downs, Kathleen had two unexpected spiritual experiences. Once, she was sitting in the backyard smoking and she heard an inner voice which told her to stop smoking. For some reason which she didn't understand, she obeyed the voice. She threw out her cigarettes and never smoked again. A little while later, again in a quiet place, she heard an even more surprising voice asking her if she would give her life to God. She said, "Yes" but knew not why. Nor, I think, did she realise the enormity of that commitment. Her response was instinctive. Not long after this, Kathleen noticed that she was not well. Eventually, she went to the doctor to be told, at the age of forty-nine, that she had incurable advanced cancer which was too progressed to benefit from treatment and that she should put her affairs in order. This she did, amidst the expected fear and grieving. She was very worried about her family members, particularly, her thirteen-year-old boy.

What happened next is most interesting. Kathleen became very accepting of her forth-coming death. She sincerely surrendered her life to God. She became peaceful, happy, joyous, and loving. She was still very ill and bed-ridden. For many months, this continued. Every day she had visitors bringing flowers, prayers, and good wishes. Her grown-up children said that when they visited her, there was always a line of people to see her. People loved to be in that peaceful, happy, beautiful, and blessed environment. After some months, Kathleen began to spend short periods in the living room. These became longer until she started to feel well again. She went back to the doctor expecting him to say that the cancer had shrunk. The doctor, in amazement, told her it had completely disappeared.

Healing is the natural result of raising the level of our consciousness so that it is more closely aligned with spiritual reality. By accepting her supposed upcoming death, Kathleen was able to lift herself to a calm and peaceful spiritual state. This allowed the healing to occur. She became sincerely accepting and happy, genuinely surrendering her life to God without reservation. Kathleen's story is a beautiful example of humility and surrender and the resulting healing that spontaneously occurred. God does not want us to suffer. So much of our suffering is self-imposed, brought on by fear, repressed hatred, blame, selfishness, and the great down-fall of mankind – ignorance. With devotion and introspection, we can not only understand ourselves and life so much more but we can be spared many of its pitfalls. Those that still come our way, we accept with as much grace as possible. After all, to know that we are loved by

God brings great comfort and makes life a pleasure and a joy.

Karmic Propensities

In healing, one must also consider the destiny of the person and the karma that the person carries. To say that we accept God's will for us is to include these two conditions. Life is complex. It is a whole intricate arrangement and interconnectedness of thought-producing effect, karma, destiny, and evolution. We do our part and hope that our problem heals; and if not, we keep going and surrender everything to God. We cannot dump the body or our problems before the Divine and demand to have it fixed up in a certain way. Nor can we berate ourselves with accusations of spiritual incompetence for not doing a better job of healing. *"If I was spiritual enough, I would be able to fix this."* Acceptance, patience, and humility are foundational. We put less importance on the problem and leave it in the hands of God. In reading the lives of the saints, we see that they all had major challenges of some sort. In the end, our spiritual state is, by far, the thing that is of most importance. Sometimes, things improve when we are not looking.

Attitude of Heart

Of all the qualities that make for a happy, healthy life and a progressive spiritual path, forgiveness is one of the most basic and important. Genuine forgiveness is not a common attitude of heart. It requires too much honesty and too little ego for the average person. It is a deep and solitary process known to the individual and God. Its ramifications are highly beneficial and, sometimes, miraculous. To have an ongoing practice of forgiveness is to extend one's health, beauty, and agelessness; ever increasing one's ability to face life with freshness and energy as one grows in wisdom and loses the burden of resentment. If one learns to become aware of hidden resentments and releases them then one will glow with lightness all through the years. The passing of years will have minimal effect as it is the accumulation of hurt, not the passing of years, which ages people most rapidly.

Transformative Commitment

The commitment to forgive everyone, in all situations, without exception, including ourselves, is an intensely transformative commitment. The nature of forgiveness is such that it cannot be pretended or intellectualised. It is a practice which involves deep surrender to God and sincere humility. Surrender and humility are the two qualities which will advance our evolution most significantly. The practice of forgiveness brings quietness, stillness, peace, and happiness. If we want to be happy, we must be willing to let go of that which is most painful to us. The ego will put up a vicious fight, reminding us of how justified we are in holding onto all those things. The ego gets its life force from such resentments and so it is hardly going to co-operate with its own demise. However, with a sincere desire for happiness and peace, one finds the ability to let things go. The end result more than compensates for any temporary discomfort.

We must be honest with ourselves. When honesty is cultivated to a sufficient extent then we begin the process of looking at everything that we are upset about with a willingness to let it go. When we consciously enter the path of forgiveness, we initially work diligently on all our current matter. We do not have to choose what to work on. The soul does that for us automatically. The higher Self instinctively tries to heal itself. In this way, we gradually improve the state of our current experience of life so that we are not carrying around heavy bundles of hurt in our mind, heart, and body. The process is beautiful in its simplicity. Healing is inevitable. The time it takes is directly proportionate to our sincerity. The more sincere we are, the more honest we will be with ourselves and the more humble we will be. It is a sacred and holy process.

Nothing is Left Hidden

Within our daily spiritual practices, we cultivate a desire to bring forgiveness to everything which comes up as a sticking point. All annoyances and resentments are brought to the table of forgiveness. In this way, we not only relieve ourselves of the burden of angry, resentful thoughts but we progress in our soul's development. Our consciousness becomes more refined. This is the way to God. Reading books and doing courses is well and good at certain stages of our development. However, it alone will never get us very far. The true practice is very inward, individual, moment-by-moment. It is transformative, radical, reaching deep into every corner of our very being. Nothing is left hidden. Nothing is withheld.

It seems difficult enough to forgive the small things in life but how do we forgive the larger things, those things that we feel so justified about? One of the sayings in Alcoholics Anonymous is *There are no justified resentments.* Don't you find it interesting that in healing the lives of those addicted to substances, the release of resentments is a requirement of progress? Certainly, those first attending A.A. find the idea preposterous. However, the idea is so powerful for all who continue with the path of healing that it slowly becomes part of the fabric of life.

Freedom in Forgetting

If all else fails, we can be like the sloth in the Disney movie, *Ice Age*.

> The sloth discovered that his good friend, Diego the tiger, had been planning to betray him. Instead of carrying a grudge and seeking revenge, he said to his friend, "Ah, Diego, you know I am too lazy to carry a grudge!"

Forgetting saves us a lot of stress and emotional turmoil. It gives us back our freedom. In the end, life is as it is. Many things seem to be unfair and unexplainable. We only have to look at the world media to see how unfair things can really become. However, if we don't focus on what other people should or shouldn't be doing and if we are grateful for the gift of life then our grievances have a tendency to fade into their native nothingness.

There is a well-known story of Buddha's radiant forgiveness.

> One day, while moving around the countryside speaking of enlightenment, one of his detractors spat at him. He did nothing. A favourite disciple became enraged by the offence and asked Buddha why he let such an ignorant person do that. Buddha replied, "If a man spits at me, it is like spit-

ting into the sky. It will all come back into his own face."

This is karma. No one gets away with anything. Let God keep track of the karma score. It is far less tedious that way. We let Life judge itself. Life is wiser than we can be. One cannot interfere with or manipulate the laws of Life. They are part of existence and cannot be altered or deceived. It is best to let Truth, itself, be the guide.

Continuum of Evolution

Every thought and every deed is forever recorded in the invisible history of life and cannot help but come back to us in kind. In fact, that is how we evolve. We pay for our mistakes by suffering. We are rewarded for our progress through added happiness. It is not that God punishes or rewards us. It is the natural and inevitable working of life, the unavoidable consequences that will always return to us. We do not have to punish our so-called enemies. We do not have to punish ourselves for our own mistakes. The resulting suffering is enough punishment and will ensure our eventual progress. Self-healing is based on a willingness to understand our own vulnerabilities and weaknesses, and then to forgive them all. If we knew better, we would do better. There is an inbuilt innocence intrinsic to our nature as part of our human existence. It is the child within which causes us such problems and refuses to grow up. We acknowledge the truth about God's child, the higher innate innocence of all beings.

To forgive oneself does not, of course, negate the need to undo mistakes. True forgiveness desires to make things right. Making things right is not equivalent to guilt. The need to undo mistakes cannot be replaced by guilt. In fact, being immobilised by guilt is an avoidance of fixing things up. It makes one powerless and gives one an excuse to remain passive and negligent. To continuously feel guilty over wrong doing is both ego-confirmatory and ineffective in correcting bad karma. Guilt is the initial spur to action. Then we act in order to correct both our thoughts and the karma, and we leave the guilt behind.

Self-Love

Lack of forgiveness towards oneself will result in an accumulation of guilt and self-loathing. The more we see the inevitability of human behaviour, given the ego's nature, the more we are able to forgive ourselves. We do our best and we keep working on our progress. We are not brutal with the ego. After all, what is a poor ego to do? It has to try and survive. So, we forgive ourselves for this struggle between the ego and the soul. We forgive the inevitable human stupidity that we see in ourselves and in others every day. Then, we forget about it and keep our attention on the goodness of Life.

When we feel God's love and forgiveness, we naturally love and forgive ourselves. When we know that God does indeed love us, it is a small step to include others in that love. It is relatively easy to share a love which we genuinely feel we are freely given, simply by our existence. We are loved into life, as is all of manifest creation.

Discernment

Forgiveness does not mean we become weak and pathetic. It does not mean that we let anyone and everyone take over our life, property, family, state-of-mind or country without so much as a peep. Wisdom and courage are also required. We often need to protect ourselves and those we are responsible for. If there is a genuinely good reason why it is not appropriate, wise, safe or beneficial to have contact with certain people then we don't. At the practical human level, we organise our life so that we are safe from certain people. Sometimes, we just can't cope with certain people, at certain times of our life. It is important to protect our family members, friends, and projects from those who wish to harm, consciously or unconsciously.

Anyone below a certain level of consciousness or who is temporarily acting below a certain level of consciousness or who acts towards us with qualities below a certain level of consciousness cannot be reasoned with or generally influenced by qualities of goodness, ethics, love, and brotherhood. Very frequently, ethical, decent people assume that all other humans are the same as them – ethical and decent. They are not. And some people who are ethical in some situations are not in others. Some are jealous of us and will hurt us even if they are harmless to most other people. All these factors have to be taken into consideration.

Wisdom and discretion are essential to our safety. We cannot assume that all people want healing. We can pray for and forgive all but we can also know that some people do not respond to goodness. We desire healing and so we look for the good and trust in the higher spirit of those around us. We seek peace and brotherly love. However, if this is not tempered with an understanding of human nature, many serious errors can occur.

Spiritual Evolution

One morning at the coffee shop, my coffee arrived with the word *love* inscribed in the froth. A simple act, but sweet and uplifting. Little acts of goodwill help to soothe the pain of human hurt and ease the complexities of ongoing existence.

All life is on a continuum. Everyone is at a different level of consciousness which means we are all at a different point in our spiritual development. How we each think, speak, and act is directly related to our level of consciousness and we can do very little else except by gradual evolution. So, what sense does it make to blame someone else or ourselves for being where we are?

Thinking, at any stage, is directly related to how life is perceived at that level. It is not black and white, good and bad. It is gradations. What looks fine from one level, looks dreadful from a higher level. What is blissful at a higher level is boring and incomprehensible at a lower level. What is satisfying and no problem at one level is totally unacceptable when outgrown. All is relative.

As life is a continuum of evolution, it makes sense to remove the blaming and self-righteousness. We are all approaching life in a way that is understandable at any given level of consciousness. This sort of compassion is not about being virtuous or self-sacrificing. It is simply acknowledging a truth that is everywhere. We are compassionate because there is no other intelligent way to be.

So often, people walk through life with blinkers on, being totally absorbed in their own considerable problems and not really noticing the struggles that others have. It is very easy to be judgemental about things that happen to other people that we assume would never happen to us. Life is complex and many things can happen that we would not expect.

Losing a sense of judgement is a reliable indicator that we have dedicated ourselves to emotional maturity and spiritual growth. It helps us to move forward in life, accepting the altered routes and enthusiastically embracing new terrains.

Who did what to who

is a trifling matter compared with preserving a stable and peaceful mind. In this way, all change will be to our benefit and will be an advancement in our capacity to fulfil our potential. Life will reward us with love, respect, and success.

Finding Our Prize

Spiritual progress is not a result of the human mind or will. One cannot make oneself think or desire any spiritual thing. It is the result of past lessons and karma which combine to give us the momentum to make certain progressive decisions. We are born already with a certain level of consciousness and a desire to achieve a certain amount of spiritual growth. It is pointless to criticise spiritually unaware people because if they could be different, they would be. It is also pointless to take personal credit for one's spiritual integrity and interest because it is simply a natural result of past spiritual work and karma. And there is, of course, a long way to go.

One can take great comfort from the fact that if one is interested in spiritual seeing, if one takes pleasure from reading or hearing uplifting and truthful spiritual ideas, if one desires to have peace, love, and happiness then one is bound to find it. The very desire is proof that one is already at a stage of consciousness where one is on a clear spiritual path that can ultimately go nowhere else but to God. With sincerity and wisdom, it can be all the more direct.

Tragedy

We are here to evolve. All life forms serve one ultimate purpose – to align themselves with the good, the beautiful, and the infinite. As human souls, this takes a tremendous amount of growth; much more than one short time on Earth can give. We gradually become more aligned to the higher life-force over a long period of soul evolution. What may seem a tragedy by the standard of one short lifetime is merely a page in an ongoing story which has a higher purpose and plot far beyond the momentary appearance. We can trust the Divine nature of the story with all its twists and turns.

Acceptance makes a lighter load of things that will only make sense in the end. Our view is relatively short-term. Our limited sense of life is not the confines of a limitless Intelligence. We must remember the true essence of life – indestructible, immaterial, completely safe, and utterly untouchable. We are spiritual, not physical, beings. That does not change with either birth or death. It remains constant. Our true essence is intangible, bodiless, and ethereal.

For a short amount of time, we enjoy the beauty of being human and, also, grow from the inevitable pain of human life. The life of our soul lives a much purer existence. It does not suffer. We can never be torn apart from that which we love. Human life forms are not lost. The deep human bonds of love are forever forged in infinity. They simply change form every now and again, waiting to re-form into another chapter of our existence. Loved homes and businesses are also never lost. Material form may crumble but the heart of a home and the service of a business are invisible. They are easily reformed out of the tiniest of material substance to yet again house the same love and service.

No Laws but God's

When fears rise supreme, we remember that in spite of any picture to the contrary, our greatest protection is to understand that we are under no laws but God's. God's laws are love, strength, order, and harmony. They are invisible, yet, mighty and powerful. They silently but surely bring the hand of peace and order into seeming turmoil and fear. They are an unseen medicine bringing quiet, sure healing, and stability. Such is our mainstay through all of the human experience. To the extent that we understand that we are under no laws but God's, our fear disappears. It is not possible to be afraid when all the Universe and beyond is working under the infinitely good orchestration of the Divine.

Armed with these simple truths, we radiate a firm and unshakeable knowledge that there is, in every situation, an inner and higher reality which is unmarred by the many, different human dramas. We help those around us with our serenity and trust. Each one of us is loved greatly. No person or event or anything on Earth or beyond can take this from us.

Quotes

Make one's life a living prayer by intention, alignment, humility, and surrender.

— David Hawkins

Spiritual energy can exhibit the emergence of healings when karmic propensities are favourable.

— David Hawkins

Choose to be unconditionally compassionate and forgiving to all of life in all its expressions.

— David Hawkins

All resentments are petulant self-indulgences of sentimentality, emotionality, and melodrama.

— David Hawkins

Everything in the universe, even the smallest thought, gives off a calibratable energy or vibratory track. These vibratory events are recorded permanently in the energy field of consciousness which is beyond time and space.

— David Hawkins

Self-healing is the willingness to love and forgive ourselves, to look at our vulnerability and call it our humanness. It is the capacity to love our humanness for its weaknesses, errors, and foibles in order to see that within this humanness, as mistaken as it might be, there is a primordial, intrinsic innocence.

— David Hawkins

Forgiveness is the attribute of the strong.

— Mahatma Gandhi

Forgetfulness is a form of freedom.

— Kahlil Gibran

Chapter 5

Simple Pleasures

Home

Little Oakey

My grandfather, Michael John Pope, was a pioneer farmer in outback New South Wales, Australia. He built his small, four-room home, *Little Oakey*, from the creek-stones of the area. Behind the house was a wattle and daub (clay) kitchen and cellar. In that little home, with his wife Mary Jane, he raised five children in, what would be considered by today's standards, primitive isolation. One of his daughters, my aunt, describes Little Oakey,

Our home was situated on Little Oakey Creek; a very pretty spot surrounded by lovely oak trees and mountains. There were paddocks, a creek running by the orchard, haystacks, a vegetable garden, wells dug in both gardens, wildflowers growing all around the flats, and a spring where we all swam. I always loved our home and dreamed about it many times and had happy times when going to school.

— Ann Pope

My mother was the youngest child in her family. She and the other children would walk or ride by horseback to a tiny country school miles away. The school was a one-room, one-teacher school with a chimney that constantly smoked. The students consisted of brothers, sisters, and cousins. Sometimes, the Macquarie River would flood and they would cross the river by boat if it was too high to cross over on horseback. On weekends, my mother and her same-aged niece would cross the river and walk several miles to deliver mail, bread, and parcels to Little Oakey. On Saturday evenings, Grandfather would get out his concertina and play for the extended family.

To visit the nearest town to shop was a rare event. The Post Office had the only phone in the district. A great highlight was going to the local dances. However, getting there was not such an easy task as another aunt describes,

We had to ride in the back of our father's truck; regal in our ball gowns and all our finery. One drawback was eight gates in eight miles to open; a fifteen-mile journey in all. At times, it was a very cold ride. At other times, it would be dry and dusty. Wet weather was another obstacle. There were several creek crossings to ford. The big hill with its slippery red clay was, sometimes, too difficult for our vehicle to get up, even if we all piled out and pushed. So, often, it was safer to stay home and suffer the disappointment.

— Beryl Lang

Grandfather worked his sheep grazing property from dawn to dusk, as is the way with farmers. His son, also a farmer, was given two Italian prisoners-of-war, Giacomo and Lorenzo, to help with the workload during World War II. The Italians would have been not much more than boys, perhaps twenty or so. The family treated them with care and respect and became very fond of them, much to the disapproval of some local families. They slept in the stables but, remember, the main house was tiny and wouldn't have had a whole lot more comfort than the stables. Anyway, a safe stables was far superior to a life-and-death war-field. When winter came, they were both knitted a jumper which they wore every year until the end of the war.

Sometimes, the two "prisoners" were sent off with guns and children in tow to catch rabbits for the day. Hardly wartime behaviour with the prisoners in charge of the weapons and with care of the children! The family kept in contact with the Italian men and visited them, many years later, on a once-in-a-lifetime European trip. Our spiritual heritage is brothers with linked arms, not brothers in armament.

Such was life in the outback. It was and, essentially, still is harsh, relentless, and intensely beautiful. It becomes part of the soul and is embedded into one's psyche as primal home.

Solitude and Civilisation

If possible, it is best to have a balance between the civilisation of city life and the solitude of country living. Too much solitude and we can become isolated and lose the benefit of human culture, progress, and communication. Too much urban life and we lose our spiritual essence and our fundamental native homeostasis.

Many people instinctively withdraw to the country or the seaside when they feel the noise of city life is drowning out the quiet inner voice of peace. The country does what the city cannot. It quietens the mind and brings simplicity into one's life. The city does what the country cannot. It enlivens the mind and brings culture into one's life. If possible, we try to engage with both and benefit from the well-roundedness of a complete experience of all that life has to offer.

Get Back on the Horse

Some years ago, I went horse riding with my then fifteen-year-old son while on holiday. Horses are a part of life in the outback. My horse-riding skills are not like my country relatives but horses are, nevertheless, not strangers. All was going well with our ride until the very end when I closely avoided an accident with a bolting horse. I was on the bolting horse. Although the accident was avoided, I noticed that for the coming week I had a growing dread of our approaching next ride. I started telling myself that I must be too old to ride. I tried to escape from going to the next ride but my son insisted I go. So, I started to work on the fear.

For the next few days, I could hear my male relatives' voices telling me, in rather gruff tone, *Just get back on the horse.* There is a common wisdom among horsemen and women that if you have a fall, if at all possible, you must get back on straight away. They know that if you don't, the fear can grow to such proportions that you may never get on again. Another common saying is,

If you can count how many times you have fallen off a horse then you are not a real rider.

Falling and failing are an inbuilt part of the whole thing. There are many times in life when we fall and fail. Sometimes, it is our own fault. Sometimes, it is not. It may be the horse, someone else, the circumstance, the timing, human nature, destiny, or a complex problem of considerable proportions. In all these situations, we need courage. Courage to get back on that horse. Courage to keep going. Courage to try again. Courage is the basis of all growth and if we are not growing then we are probably going backwards. So, get back on that horse and live your life as you are meant to.

Cottage by the Sea

At one stage, we bought an old, fibro fisherman's cottage in Lorne. Lorne is a small seaside town surrounded by National Park. It is the spectacular but, generally, quiet meeting point of forest and stunning coastline. Lorne's normal population is one thousand people. During the summer holiday month of January, it swells to twenty thousand and then peace returns, once again, to the beautiful, little town. The house had an overgrown garden with a jumble of fencing to keep various animals safe over the years. It had an original orchard where the trees had not been tended for many years. All was a delight for creative unfoldment.

The previous owner of the cottage, Lenny, was seventeen when he built the three-bedroom home with his wife in 1939. Lenny lived in his home for over seventy years. Such homes, as simple as they may be, have the energy field of long-term love. No grand, new, magnificent building can acquire such an auric field. It is the accumulated result of decades of domestic family life.

Likewise, such gardens, as overgrown and unkempt as they may be at the end, have a secret reservoir of beauty underneath the weeds, dead branches, and rubbish. Decades of loving human care breed into plants an invisible quality which waits to be reignited by the loving care of a new guardian. Such things are folk law. Is it not the sweet mystery of the archetypal *secret garden*? A garden once adored then lost through misfortune, tragedy, or neglect and then, once again, found and restored through healing, grace, and the unceasing pull towards life and restoration.

Focus on What is Alive

Our garden plants can be so resilient. Without fail, they reappear each year with the same, often, greater determination to play their part and make their little spot of the world a place of beauty. Sometimes, they are splendid for a while and then they disappear, never to return. They only came to shine briefly. Perhaps, we did not give them what they needed. Perhaps, it was not meant to be. Perhaps, it was not reasonably possible. They may have required more attention than we were able or willing to give. They may have been on a different wavelength to us and not in sync with our own gardening style. So, we graciously let them go. Many an experienced gardener will wisely advise,

Don't worry about what dies. Focus on what is alive.

Such is a good approach to life.

Gardens are as different as each one of us. I love cottage gardens. At their best, they are bordering on the brink of chaos. There is, however, an invisible, underlying, loose order. Both garden and gardener are joined in a beautifully crafted patchwork of creative energy which is forever fresh and green. The free-spirited order of a cottage garden is sweet, homely, unpretentious, honest, and reassuring.

To have the good fortune of a garden and the luxury of a little time to work in it is a wonderful blessing. Gardening is a simple pleasure and, as such, it encourages the formation of patience, humility before the power of nature, and appreciation for what the unfolding of destiny brings to our life. It helps us to practise the release of demanding expectations. The qualities of wonder and delight are fostered. It feeds our bond with the multitudinous forms of life that call Earth home.

We can learn to see the beauty and wholeness which is always around us. Nothing is lacking. Timing is precisely right. All life is sacred and all life forms should be honoured. They are worthy of being here, simply by virtue of the fact that they are here.

It is often the simple things in life which bind us as sisters and brothers, the inevitable shared struggles and joys of human life. Simple pleasures and common goodness ignite and fuel our humanity. The renewal of spring, the surrender of autumn, a genuine smile, an unexpected and sincere compliment, an expression of spontaneous warmth, a forgiving look from a previously angry person. These things tell us that there is hope and that life is evolving as it should.

Quotes

There is nothing as important when making ready for the day, as an early morning period of stillness, wherein to make sure that the Truth, and the Truth only, controls our consciousness...we can be assured that Love will guide us, that success will ultimately crown every endeavour, for all things work together for good.

— Nora Holm

Gratitude is the door to joy.

— Thomas Hora

If the only prayer you said was thank-you, that would be enough.

— Meister Eckhart

Indeed, [the garden] is the purest of human pleasures. It is the greatest refreshment to the spirits of man.

— Francis Bacon

Love giveth to the least spiritual idea might, immortality, and goodness, which shine through all as the blossom shines through the bud.

— Mary Baker Eddy

In the sweetness of friendship let there be laughter, and sharing of pleasures. For in the dew of little things, does the heart find its morning and is refreshed.

— Kahlil Gibran

Chapter 6

Silence

A Source of Great Strength

Quiet

As a child and teenager, I was quiet. Apart from a naturally introspective personality, the quietness was primarily driven by fear. This was deliberately overcome when I made a conscious decision at age fifteen to stop living in social fear and started reaching out to my school peers in a proactive way.

One day, while sitting in class at school, I asked myself,

Why is it that some girls are popular and seem happy and confident and I, on the other hand, am far from that?

I looked around at the girls, searching for the answer. My eyes fell upon a girl who was confidently engaged in a conversation with one of her friends. The friend was genuinely enjoying her company. My classmate looked balanced, carefree, and engaged with life. I then asked myself,

What is this girl doing that makes her companion enjoy her company?

I looked closer and for the first time, I could see what it was. The girl was looking outward not inward. My classmate was reaching out to her peers in an enthusiastic, positive, and lively way. She wasn't waiting for someone to talk to her as was my general approach to peer relationships. She was taking the first step and carrying the conversation along in a calm and bright manner.

Ah, outwards not inwards! That is the secret, I thought. *Make an effort. Be brave. Reach out. Stop being such a scaredy-cat.*

From that moment, something important in my life changed. As soon as the bell rang to end the class, I made my first, faltering move in a new direction. I turned to the nearest girl and asked her with way too much enthusiasm how her day had been. Although looking somewhat taken aback at my no longer silent voice and the exaggerated enthusiasm with which I spoke, she nevertheless spoke with interest in the ensuing conversation about her day. Such was the beginnings of a bright and bubbly personality and my growing understanding of how to win friends and influence people.

The whole thing gained momentum and went from strength to strength so that it was mastered by the time I was twenty-two. I had more friends than I needed and I could usually attract the attention of most people who I had an interest in befriending. Seven years of practising to overcome shyness and fear and I reached a point of graduating from the course in advanced interpersonal proficiency.

Once mastered, I utterly lost interest in it. I began the serious quest of spiritual, not interpersonal, mastery. I said goodbye to the bubble that had served me so well for seven years and returned to the quieter persona. However, this time it would not be driven by fear but, eventually, by a conscious, calm equilibrium. I had only just opened the gate to this new domain. At twenty-two, I indeed had a long way to go. However, like my previous challenge at fifteen, it was step by step. We just take that first faltering step.

Peaceful Centre

A balanced, inner calmness radiates from a peaceful centre. It neither craves others' approval nor rejects others' presence. It neither pulls towards nor pushes away. It has a reverent attitude towards life and all its inhabitants. It has compassion for the inevitable weaknesses of the human condition. It has nothing to gain from others' approval. It is not self-seeking. It is not needy, grabbing or manipulative. It embodies gracious respect for everything beautiful including other human souls. It has a lively freedom, a happy composure, a quick and engaging wit, and an intelligent, interested, and interesting mental attitude.

Some people have a seemingly quiet life but they are noisy inside. Some people have a seemingly busy life but they have a quietness within. To lessen the inner noise we can develop self-awareness, introspection, and stillness. We grow in solitude. We need quiet times. They make our life happier and less problematic. They move us closer to glowing health, agelessness, peace, prosperity, clear thinking, inspired ideas, harmonious and interesting relationships, and effective problem solving. They secure our personal and spiritual progress. As we become more conscious through the practice of quiet times, we progressively lose the problems of illness, stress, confusion, and relationship breakdowns. By having quiet times, we start to wake up.

Dedicated Quiet Time

The *quiet time* has several requirements:

1. **Solitude** – we must be alone. Our psyche will never go into the recesses of our deepest thoughts if we are not in the solitary presence of ourselves and God only. Thoughts will not rise from the depth of our unconscious without clear permission and a suitable mental environment. Unconscious thoughts need our undivided attention before they dare to show their hidden form.

2. **Time** – a least half an hour. An hour is wonderful. One grows to love the time although, at first, it can be uncomfortable. Those who are very dedicated spiritual students, eventually, extend the quality of consciousness that they attain in their quiet time to their entire day and even to their night while asleep. It is what is meant by *pray without ceasing*. It becomes an effortless, aware state of mind that remains constant within the developed practitioner.

3. **Space** – dedicate a space of your own where you will be undisturbed. If you have your own room then that is fabulous. If it is a beautiful

and peaceful room with a lovely, natural outlook then you could ask for nothing better. However, anything will do. If there is no space at all, go into the garden or go for a walk. Your walk will be a walking meditation, a time for reflection and healing. Don't use the time walking to the railway station on the way to work as your only quiet time because your mind will be naturally focused on the day's activities. Walking to the station is an added bonus of quiet, not your dedicated quiet time. Of course, if you live alone then your life, at this point, will have much solitude. Make the most of it for your personal growth because you do not know how long it will last. Someone who works on him or herself will inevitably make much progress and will be in demand with requests to participate in life in all sorts of ways. How we respond is dependent on our preferences, needs, and destiny.

4. **Go into our thoughts** – the whole purpose of a quiet time is to give our mind the conditions it needs to allow unconscious thoughts to rise to the surface of our mind. It is our unconscious thoughts which lead and form our life, far more than our conscious ones. They can and do lead us into danger. They can also lead us to safety. The more we are aware of what these thoughts are, the more we become their master. It is a fool who believes he is a master of his own destiny when he does not even know his own thoughts.

5. **Face our fears** – as we go deeper into our

thoughts, we must have the courage to allow the emotions attached to them to also surface. Every unconscious, buried thought has an attached emotion. Often, it is a difficult emotion such as fear, jealousy, anger, grief, despair, loneliness, hopelessness or insecurity. These unpleasant emotions are the reason we condemned the thought to unconsciousness in the first place. We will find that if we allow both the underlying thought and the attached emotion to surface then they will lessen, heal, and transform. This is experientially verified by our own practice.

6. **Give our grievances air time** – one of the most important aspects of a quiet time is to give our repressed anger a voice. The quiet time is the right place to express anger. Make sure no one can hear you. Swear, stamp your feet, throw things, hurl your worst insults, and be totally irrational. After all, the unconscious mind is, by nature, irrational. It lifts the repressed anger. Most of us are horrified by the mass of anger which lies inside us. It seems so childish and so unreasonable. It is. Remember it is the child talking and screaming with rage. Give it space to surface and it will release the pent-up energy and one day disappear. It leads to forgiveness and healing. Persistent practice of releasing this energy makes our heart freer and lighter.

Commonality of Thought

Although we each believe our thoughts are specific and personal to ourselves, in fact, our thoughts, fears, and desires are normal to all egos and are commonly shared. In this way, it is relatively easy to read the thoughts of most humans with just a few subtle cues. Thoughts tend to run along the same worn tracks leading to the same worn conclusions. Combining this knowledge with an understanding of the types of thoughts that individuals at different levels of consciousness will gravitate towards will, with experience, lead to becoming a most astute mind reader.

Seeing the commonality of human thought helps us to view our ego tendencies in a less personal and more universal way. It relieves guilt and gives lightness to the path by virtue of the collective and general nature of human experience. The ego is a shared human problem and its dissolution is a benefit to all mankind. Human life is inevitably filled with many hurts and injustices. We do not live in a world of enlightened beings, nor are we enlightened ourselves. We live in a world where most people are struggling, unhappy, and having numerous problems of all sorts.

Spiritual Withdrawal

At every stage of consciousness above a certain basic level, there appears to be a sweet spot in the middle where all seems to work relatively well. A soul can remain in that nice place for a whole lifetime if that is what is destined. We all know people who are happy and content at their own varying levels of consciousness. To move into the next stage of development, the soul will have to go through an uncomfortable period of struggle. When change is imminent, the restlessness of the individual will force the person to break from the comfort of the known into the unknown of new territory.

Some people will reach a certain point in their growth and they will wish to withdraw from the world. It is not the withdrawal of an antisocial or fearful person running away from the world. Short periods of withdrawal are, of course, beneficial to everyone. However, this type of withdrawal is for the purpose of deep, spiritual transformation. It is the withdrawal of someone who is, generally, already competent in the world. Otherwise, our shortcomings will rise to pull us back into the world where they will be thrown at us again for educational reasons. Withdrawal is not really a choice, nor is it difficult. The attachment to the world will have already diminished and the person will crave the solitude that, at that stage, is the only way they can remain connected to that which they seek.

A Fresh Universe

After a serious fall in 1866, Mary Baker Eddy was bedridden and those around her feared for her survival. However, not only did she survive but from this near-tragedy came the birth of Christian Science. The fall was at the end of a long line of sufferings as Mary had suffered from many illnesses and problems for most of her life. Having reached despair, on the third day of being bedridden, Mary had a sudden and stunning realisation while reading her Bible,

As I read, the healing Truth dawned upon my sense; and the result was that I arose, dressed myself, and ever after was in better health than I had before enjoyed. That short experience included a glimpse of the great fact that I have since tried to make plain to others, namely, Life in and of Spirit; this Life being the sole reality of existence.

— Mary Baker Eddy

Mary needed to distil the thrilling (but still new and unclear) spiritual truths that were becoming apparent to her. She consciously withdrew from society for three years, in order to make sense of the truths and in preparation to present them to the world in a form that was worthy of their importance. In those three years, she pondered her mission, searched the Scriptures, wrote the foundation of her seminal book, and sought to clarify her teachings. The quest was calm, and the time alone was both recuperative and strengthening.

The divine hand led me into a new world of light and life, a fresh universe – old to God, but new to His 'little one'.

— Mary Baker Eddy

Semi-Invisible

Bernadette Roberts was a former Carmelite nun and modern mystic who died at eighty-seven, a few years ago, in her sleep. She entered the Carmelite monastery as a teenager and remained there as a secluded, cloistered nun for ten years. During that time, she went through *a dark night of the soul* until she reached a unitive state with God. She then re-entered the world, got a degree, married, had four children, worked as a school teacher, and all the while continued her contemplative practices.

Some thirty years after re-entering the world, she went through another, more advanced, process of losing the self. It was not sought but, she said, was brought on by God taking away her sense of herself. This naturally took her a long adjustment period – ten more years. In describing this pathway, she explained that the sense of two progressively became One. She did not take students or enter into correspondence and, other than her books, her sole public presence was through a small, annual retreat. She said that she had never had any interest in taking students and that she was too busy with family duties, anyway. She was a mystic who choose to remain *semi-invisible*.

Rite of Passage

Some type of separation or seclusion is, for some of us, a necessary rite of passage. When we see through the self-confirmatory nature of most human interaction, we can decide to refrain from participating in it for some time. One must learn to tolerate and live with the silence, before one is ready to talk the talk of the angels. The silence extends our capacity to become one with God. For a few people, the silence remains in the form of seclusion. For all, it remains internally and is regarded as precious. It, sometimes, requires the silence of withdrawal to spiritually work through some inner milestones. What other people think about this is only of concern because of our love for others and our compassion for their inability to understand what we may be doing. However, the focus is not on what others think of us but on how we can fulfil our spiritual potential and help the world. There can be a transitory conflict between spiritual evolution and the pull towards that which is conventional, acceptable, and normal human behaviour. The world, as ignorant as it is, accepts very little deviation from its often ridiculous and unfounded ideas of normalcy.

As the underlying motives of typical human behaviour become clearer to us, we can be shocked and disconcerted by the selfish, inconsiderate, disingenuous, and frequently harmful intentions of routine, daily interaction. All of this is not apparent to the average man or woman who is engrossed in accustomed life without much awareness. After discovering this, we can become rather dismissive of all human interaction and find it stupid, pointless, and destructive. Our tolerance even for fundamental, polite niceties which are considered crucial in customary, day-to-day convention can become rather thin. Then, for a period, we may withdraw from mainstream behaviour in order to go within and metamorphose into something else more real and good. We all know of the introverted artist, the isolated mystic, and the unsociable philosopher who have withdrawn from traditional, societal communication.

Nonpersonal, Intelligent Love

We may wonder if we are on the right track because, for a while, we may seem less loving than we were before. It helps to remind ourselves of the shallowness of most normal love and that we are seeking to demonstrate something better. At least, in solitude and withdrawal, one is offering a more sincere, albeit, silent and unconventional love of a nonpersonal, intelligent nature. There is no need to doubt the worth of our developing capacity to radiate a quiet, unpretentious energy field. Our goal of true, spiritual love is concerned with neither niceness nor prevailing behaviour patterns. It is a radical transition. This transformation occurs step by step. Mostly, it is the unexplainable and deeply welcomed grace of God. It has its own timing and evolution. We keep offering up everything not in accord with the desired goodness we seek. And we are kind to ourselves, allowing as much solitude as needed, knowing that our worth to the world is growing daily in a precious and uncommon manner.

The withdrawal creates an environment for the, mostly, involuntary diminishing of the ego. The person loses interest in the normal worldly goings-on. One will have little or no interest in the media and will probably actively avoid it because of its negative impact on one's consciousness. In some cases, one can go for years without knowing even the most basic information about world affairs. One keeps going forward until, quite surprisingly, one realises that the valley has been passed and a lightness and freedom comes back into one's being. One has to wait until the Greater Forces have dissolved the ego enough for the precious Light to take up residence within one's being to the extent that is required for that individual at that time in their evolution.

Solitary Confinement

The period of isolation may be deceptive in appearance. A person can live an, apparently, solitary lifestyle but the mind is full of interaction and busy noise. That is not solitude. It is a crowd. On the other hand, one can live the appearance of a normal life but, unbeknown to onlookers, be transgressing through a self-imposed solitary confinement.

In my own case, my most intensive period of isolation was during my late twenties. However, this was totally unknown to anyone at the time. How was this possible, particularly given that I had two young children and was married?

My young family had moved countries from Australia to England. My Australian relatives and friends would have assumed I was living a normal life in England but they just didn't happen to hear much about it. This was a good arrangement because, certainly, one doesn't want to worry people unnecessarily. I deliberately kept to myself during my three years in England because I was involved in this inner work. My husband worked long hours in a demanding CEO position and spent many weeks travelling abroad and was not aware of what I was doing. My days were spent in the company of two very little children. As we communicated quite naturally in a telepathic manner, as many mothers do with their little children, there was little need for speech. It was silence, indeed. The solitary period extended more than the three years in England. It had started some time before then and continued for a year after our return to Australia.

Then, all of a sudden, life took one of those unexpected and totally transforming turns and the children and I happily threw ourselves into the busy life of a lively community. I was back in the bustling marketplace, after returning from the hermitage caves. By now, however, the solitude had taken up permanent residence within my being.

In the Midst of Humanity

In travelling through this spiritual territory, one does one's part to the best of one's ability but it is not really a process that can be greatly altered by individual will. The work comes from Beyond. Eventually, we come out the other end of our withdrawal with a renewed interest in other people and a rekindled desire for participation in life.

To most people, we seem more or less the same, except that we are more direct and honest and we may seem a little disinterested in normal things. However, inside we are totally different. Driven by God's unconditional love, we have a great deal more strength, courage, wisdom, and equanimity. We do not open our mouth without the express desire to be of service in contributing something of value to that which is around us. It is a process well worth every little pain. For a rare, few, great ones, the road ultimately leads to the fulfilment of their spiritual potential as a master or rishi. Their energy holds the world together.

In the beginning, being a stranger to the world can feel alone. As spiritual beings, to some extent, we are ever a stranger to normal human life. We are in the world but not of it. When the humanness has diminished enough and the human karma worked through enough, the alone feeling evaporates, never to return. In fact, it becomes apparent that it would be impossible to ever feel alone again as one is intimately connected to a thriving life-force. We feel intrinsically related to everyone. We have a deep solitariness but we can never be lonely because there can no longer be any separation from God. We are more a part of humanity than ever before because we see all as of God. We are all here together, joined irrevocably in the evolution of humanity both individually and collectively.

It could be said that we become so much a stranger that we disappear and find ourselves reborn in the midst of humanity, which is quite a paradox. What remains is invisible, wordless, comforting, strong, and soft. It is every beautiful leaf, every moving human emotion, and every breath of every living thing. It is everything, yet, it is nothing. It grows silently and steadily. We are already it, and It is already us. We continue to go forward with our spiritual practices and these practices increasingly envelop us in loveliness. We come out the other side as a transparent being, nameless but with the mark of God. One could wish for nothing more.

The Mystic

Some time ago, it was mentioned to me that I may like to read St. Teresa of Avila's autobiographical book, *The Book of My Life*. I ordered the book and forgot about it. I knew almost nothing about St. Teresa, at that time, not even that she was a Carmelite nun. St. Teresa is an esteemed Catholic mystic and contemplative of the 16th century. Just before I received the book, I had the following dream:

> After a certain sequence of events, I went to live in
> an enclosed Carmelite Order. I saw no one for
> fifteen years except the other nuns. I was cared for
> simply and spent all my time in prayer. (Later on, I
> realised that this was in line with St. Teresa's prefer-
> ence for monastic life.) It was extremely enjoyable
> and I became less and less mortal and more and
> more ethereal. It was a complete and utter pleasure.

The feeling in the monastery was exquisitely beautiful.

After the fifteen years, it was time to go and see someone in the world. I watched myself doing this. However, by this time my body was not very visible so I wore long, flowing garments to cover it. I had a large glow around me – very light and beautifully luminescent. It radiated about two feet from my body. I wore a cloak over my head which seemed to bring the glow next to me so that no one noticed it. I no longer needed to walk but could glide over the surface of the path.

I found talking very burdensome, as I normally communicated telepathically. However, I had to talk to a few people in order to get to the person I needed to see. At one point there was a problem, as those people wanted to know my name. I did not want to tell them my name and so I told them tele-pathically, "You are now happy to let me see the person I want to see and will ask no further ques-tions." This they did instantly, although they knew not why. When I got to the person I wished to see, there was an instant recognition and all was well.

Then the dream was over.

Favours from God

St. Teresa was a saint of visions. She was well known for her mystical experiences or *favours from God* as she called them. Although mystical experiences are favours in that they are gifts, God has no favourites and we are all loved equally. The overriding spiritual intention of Life is for everyone to fulfil their potential, find their peace, and feel the happiness of being a unique and deeply valued soul. To seek spiritual experiences is a spiritually deceptive exercise. It is the ego which wishes to be special and have proof thereof by unusual experiences.

Uplifting experiences are a pleasure and joy. However, it is the daily seeking of peace and the moment by moment practice of love, surrender, and courage which carries true spiritual weight. Such is the nature of the spiritual path. The path is not paved with unusual experiences. It is paved with consistent, conscious mental and spiritual alertness and goodness in our heart. It is this practice which will bring us our goal of true happiness.

Living in Two Realms

As spiritual students living in the world, we cultivate an inner, silent stillness through the practice of contemplation or awareness. Behind the normal goings-on of everyday life there is a consistent wakefulness; an awareness of what we are thinking, what other people are thinking, and what is the spiritual truth of any given situation. We live in two realms. One is the practical, left-brained, human realm. The other is the etheric, inspired, right-brained, spiritual realm. We are in the world but not of it. We pray without ceasing by virtue of our dedication to the still, inner awareness of God.

End of Thinking

When the mind becomes quiet, thinking ceases and is replaced by a certain inner knowing. Each moment is lived with presence. Each moment is, in itself, the entirety of existence. All that needs to be known is there. St. Teresa said that in the higher states of prayer one becomes incapable of thinking. All is God, infinite Good, and there is none else. We surrender to Love. We become nothing. We become all. No past, no future, no longing, no mind. We could even forget who we are, forget our name, yet, we are at home in everything, everywhere. It is, somewhat, akin to the first transitional moments of waking from a restorative sleep. We are happy and peaceful, in need of nothing, and have not quite recollected all the details of our human life.

Past and Future

The past and the future annoy, worry, and unsettle the soul with their endless ranting. The path of prayer is the disappearance of the ego into submergence with God. When the soul is engaged in deep communion with God, the normal ego functioning of thought is greatly retarded and the individual loses himself in the wordless, thoughtless, egoless domain of spirit. Of course, one cannot function in the world like that and one would have to re-engage thought in order to participate effectively in life.

Silence is the breeding ground of harmonious, perfect action. It is also the soil in which love grows. Without silence, we can neither know ourselves, another or the depth of anything beautiful. One has to be able to tolerate seeming nothingness in order to hear the silent rhythm. It warms our heart and stretches us into beautiful forms. It is prayer and its velvety smoothness effortlessly embraces us.

Pursuit of Enlightenment

The spiritual traditions of the East are ancient, varied, and full of tried and tested spiritual practices. It seems that while the Western world has primarily focused on the advancement of modern civilisation, the Eastern world, to a large extent, has remained a culture steeped in spiritual traditions. In the latter, it is somewhat acceptable for a young adult to announce to their family that they are devoting their life to the spiritual quest and will not be pursuing the normal interests of profession, spouse, and children. In the West, if a young man or woman announces to their family and friends that they have no interest in pursuing the normal interests of life and they wish to dedicate their life to the pursuit of enlightenment, they will most likely be confronted with a most concerned family and friends who will be worried for their mental health.

Renunciation of Mental Positions

All spiritual work is, in a sense, renunciation. More than any outward lifestyle renunciations, we are renouncing the ego and, more specifically, the pay-off that the ego normally gets in life. In return, we are rewarded with the blessings of spiritual growth. We are renouncing the juice of self-confirmatory aggrandisement. In return, we are rewarded with inner peace. We are renouncing the pleasure of taking credit. In return, we are rewarded with the long-term benefits of humility. The spiritual path is an on-going series of renouncing short–term egotistic gains for long-term spiritual returns and happiness. Although frequently tempting to do otherwise, the latter is a far better choice.

Inevitably people will hurt us, other people, and themselves. In one day alone, if we look carefully, we will recognise a number of instances when someone did something, said something or insinuated something which was offensive to our fragile sense of ourselves. A harsh look, a grouchy reply, a mean remark, an uncaring attitude are all commonplace daily experiences. That is without even looking at the major hurts we carry with us all the time. Abuse, selfishness, competitiveness, betrayal, and manipulation are common themes widely held in consciousness. All of these hurts and offences gain substance from us holding onto them in thought in a very specific way.

- I think this.
- I don't like that.
- I hate that person for doing that.
- I want such and such.
- I demand something.
- I decree someone to be wrong.
- I am right.

All are mental positions.

Mental positions are the endless viewpoints we take which, in turn, determine the judgements and thoughts we will have about any given person, thing or event in life. They are the breeding ground of the ego. They are the ego's survival mechanism. They are the incessant struggle of the personal self to keep reminding us that all things relating to our personal self are of great significance, simply because of their attachment to our precious selfhood.

To practise releasing the millions of positions we hold in our mind is to draw closer to God. The ego takes great pleasure from all its highly prized positions, particularly, when it considers itself a victim. It is intensely reluctant to forego the pleasure of righteous indignation. Radical humility and surrender is the unpicking of the garment sewn together with the threads of ego positions. One releases these by dedication and devotion. The process is greatly aided by sufficient suffering which will impel us forward towards a different reality. If we persevere, we will draw closer to the very heart of Reality.

Gratitude

Gratitude is the foundation of love. We are grateful for life, every little expression of goodness, and every wonderful thing that is given to us or comes our way. Without gratitude, we cannot hear the joyful song that is forever playing underneath the appearance of normal life. Every morning when we wake, we can remember to focus our thoughts on the beauty of the day ahead. We can still our mind and remind ourselves that the mind of the Divine is guiding and protecting us. We can place our loved ones within the safety of that Divine care. We have so much to be grateful for, at very least, the wonderful opportunity that life is. Not one of us can ever be apart from the nurturing, protecting Love which sustains us in every way and always has.

Gratitude comes from humility. It leads to joy and, surprisingly, an unshakeable confidence. Our normal human consciousness constantly gravitates towards self-importance. Self-importance is not true confidence. Rather, it is counterfeit confidence and automatically leads to endless worries, desires, and fear that we will not be able to get what we need or protect that which we have already attained. With conscious effort, prayer, and the simple willingness to have an open heart, we begin to release, even if just for a moment, our own egotistic importance. We soften to the idea that we are not the creator of all things nor the grand director and producer. Rather, we are the grateful actor given our part to play. If we do so with enthusiasm, love, and happiness, all will go well, often, much beyond our expectations.

Gratitude grows from the soil of letting go and surrender. It is only possible to surrender when we are humble enough to acknowledge the authority of the Divine over our life and everything in it. We lean on the immense and unlimited resources of Life. We become lighter, brighter, and more radiant. The never-ending, normal problems and worries of life recede into the background and often disappear. Our being is filled with the loveliness of everything good and a knowing that good is naturally drawn to us and wishes to make its home within the walls of our garden.

Being Loving

Love is more than loving another person. We love the quality of love itself. We start to live in an energy field of love. Although this encompasses specific people, one who has learned to cultivate a loving presence loves regardless of the presence or absence of individual people. It is the love of being loving. Love, in its higher form, is universal, transpersonal, available to all, and driven by an unselfish desire for the good of everyone. In this way, we can even love strangers. If we understand the higher form of love, we are less burdened with the common problems of personal likes and dislikes, attachments and aversions, possessiveness, fear, and jealousy.

Recently, I overheard a young woman talking to her friend in the cafe about a man who she was interested in.

She explained with great enthusiasm, "The guy is so gorgeous. He's beautiful to look at. He has stunning, deep eyes. He is kind to everyone."

Then she said with obvious disappointment, "But you see, he's taken. He doesn't just love me, he loves everyone. He's a monk."

Both girls sighed in commiseration and then laughed.

The young woman did not realise she was describing the quality of someone who knows how to be a loving presence – gorgeous, soulful eyes, loves everyone, and loved by all in return. It is nonpersonal, nonconditional benevolence. It is a highly attractive quality.

Seeking the Sacred

I went to see the movie *Philomena* which is based on the, apparently, true story of an Irish teenage girl whose baby was taken from her by the Catholic nuns in 1952 and adopted to a wealthy American couple for one thousand pounds. Fifty years later, an unlikely match between Philomena and an emotionally struggling journalist brings healing to both in their search for Philomena's son. The real-life Philomena says,

> This is not a rally cry against the church or politics. In fact, despite some of the troubles that befell me as a young girl, I have always maintained a very strong hold on my faith.

> — Philomena

I walked home from the movie on a calm, warm evening in a small, Australian, seaside town and thought about the depth of the, largely unconscious, ties that we have to the sacred.

We reach for it when we are not looking. It is, in some form, imprinted into every cell of our body. It rushes forward at pivotal moments: tragedy, pain, death, new love, deep love, and healing. We carry the beauty and radiance of the love, courage, and healing which gives spirituality its potency. It is the whole, immense energy field of man's craving for release, guidance, forgiveness, and support. It is the innumerable ways in which that is expressed. We have an inherent longing for the sacred. We yearn for wholeness and meaning. It leads to transformation and freedom. In the end, we will neither seek it nor run away from it. It will become us and we will become that which, in a flawed manner, we now clumsily seek.

The Heart of Reality

More than one hundred years ago, while convalescing in hospital, Margaret Montague had an unexpected and beautiful experience of life as it really is. The nurses had just wheeled her outside for some fresh air. As she recalls, it was an ordinary, dingy day. Her spirits were about the same, as was generally the case for her at that time. She could not remember if the revelation came slowly or suddenly, only that she was overcome with the stunning beauty of it.

I only remember finding myself in the very midst of those wonderful moments, beholding life for the first time in all its young intoxication of loveliness, in its unspeakable joy, beauty, and importance. I saw no new thing, but I saw all the usual things in a miraculous new light – in what I believe is their true light. I saw for the first time how wildly beautiful and joyous, beyond any words of mine to describe, is the whole of life. Every human being moving across that porch, every sparrow that flew, every branch tossing in the wind, was caught in and was a part of the whole mad ecstasy of loveliness, of joy, of importance, of intoxication of life.

— Margaret Montague

Margaret's experience was originally published anonymously as *Twenty Minutes of Reality* in a newspaper of the day. One of the respondents to the article assured her that she could not only have twenty minutes of Reality but such could become the reality of her whole life. The respondent continued that with dedicated prayer, we become like the chicken breaking from its shell and stepping into the sunshine. Thus, the sunshine becomes the normal (not the exceptional) experience of life.

Another respondent explained that as a child he had grown up under the influence of a keenly religious mother. However, when he ventured out into the real world it came as quite a shock. He became sick and weak and lost all his beliefs in God and most things good. It one day occurred to him, rather surprisingly, that it might be possible that all the spiritual thought of his youth could be true, even though he had long since left it behind for rational argument. He asked God that if it was true then God would show him so. He was then overcome with a deep conviction and knowingness of spiritual existence. It left all too quickly. He prayed again that God might return. Indeed, the spiritual light did return, the more he asked. Soon he came to rely upon it as a sure law. Eventually, what he called the conviction stayed with him permanently.

Devotion

To enter a holy place which is imbued with the pleas of countless human beings and is the home of many a heartfelt prayer is a reminder of the breath of devotion. Such occasions call for the heart. Devotion is an act of the heart, not an intellectual endeavour. At best, the mind can inform us of our spiritual options and it expands our intellectual understanding of human nature. However, anything which remains as an idea of the mind is yet to be realised through actual being. Devotion is that realisation in one's being.

Devotion and prayer require very little thought. It is not that we become sentimental and overly emotional. The latter is a further act of the ego. Rather, true devotion calls for humility, calmness, serenity, a stunning appreciation of everything beautiful, an overwhelming gratitude for every sign of love, and a deep connection with all of life. Devotion is egoless. It is simple, pure, uplifting, enlivening, joyous, and it takes one out of oneself into the flow of spiritual life. It is beautiful, moving, and peaceful. A humble and sincere request to be blessed by life will ensure that it is so. No prayer ever goes unanswered. The act of prayer itself ensures that it will be heard because prayer, by its very nature, means an acceptance of the Divine order of life.

Peace

Although simple, peace is a highly evolved state of consciousness. It cannot live side-by-side with the ego. We choose one or the other. Peace is the predominant quality of spiritual advancement. The unassuming quality of peace wins the day when it comes to the soul's progression. To choose peace means that we give up the rantings and ravings, demands and hurts, wants and cravings of the personal mind. The personal self feeds off injustices, imagined injustices, complaining, conflict, excitement, drama, and all the goings-on of normal human life. At some point, when we have suffered enough or have enough wisdom, we tire of the whole thing. We sincerely prefer peace.

To choose peace means an inner commitment to humility. We let that which governs life take control of our life. It can be like falling off a cliff, not knowing if someone or something will be there to catch us. We just keep going, over the cliff, with all the faith that we can muster. We can also have faith in the many enlightened teachers who have lovingly led the way and gone before us. Low and behold, something does catch us and there grows within us the quiet, life-giving power of peace. It touches every part of our life and reminds us that we belong to Eternity.

Life is naturally going to have ups and downs, comings and goings, pleasures and hardships, joy and pain. Let us be kind to ourselves, understanding that we are here to learn. And let us be kind to others, knowing that peace is the ultimate prize of life and nothing is worth more. Simply to side with peace is to disempower the ego's hold. In so doing, the natural, beautiful, and healing rhythms of life have a chance to start singing their sweet song in our listening ear.

Surrender

Love, in any form, is always a contribution to the world. Some of our most spiritual people live simple lives unnoticed by others. The power of their prayer and their presence in the world is a very valuable contribution to humanity. Public recognition, in any area, is only for some. Given the temptation to be side-tracked by the fame and power that comes with public recognition, it is a recognition that advanced students avoid if it is not their specific calling. Humility and gratitude guarantee our safety, closeness to God, and happiness.

True spiritual students are imbued with humility, surrender, and devotion. Humility gives us access to the Divine realm. Without it, we don't have an entry pass. Surrender is the fount of healing. Devotion is love. It facilitates an inner alignment with the Divine. There is a radiant transformation of being. We become beauty, love, and being.

Grace

We surrender to God and are consumed with the Divine presence. Then all is Love, stunningly alive. The flower in the garden is not aware of its own beauty or from where it came. It just radiates purity and the wholeness of being. All that we are is surrendered to Divinity. When there is no tension between the inner being and that which is being expressed, there is grace. When we have a transparent acceptance of our soul and a simple desire to express the beauty of Life, there is no conflict of interest and grace is the apparent result.

Greatest Gift

The greatest gift we can give the world is our own evolution. Every time we rise a little higher in our understanding, our capacity to bless and silently influence the world increases substantially. Our gift to the world is the capacity of our soul to uplift, heal, and love. This is our reason for being. When all else fails, when we come to the end of the road, when we realise our capacity to orchestrate our own existence is fraught with endless problems, we say in deep and heart-felt sincerity to the Divine,

I surrender.

Surrender Prayer

I surrender all to you.
I surrender my life to you.
I will do whatever you want.
I will go wherever you want.
I will love whoever you ask me to love.
I will give up all my stupid opinions.
I will give up all my hopeless cravings.
I release my broken dreams.
I forfeit my planned futures.
I am at your mercy.
I will think no thought
or proceed with any action
which does not come from you
because You love me.

— Donna Goddard

Quotes

It is helpful to realise that the ego is impersonal; it is not unique at all. Everybody's innate ego operates about the same as that of everybody else. Unless modified by spiritual evolution, all ego/selves are self-serving, egotistical, vain, misinformed, and committed to endless gain in all its customary forms, such as moralistic superiority, possessions, fame, wealth, adulation, and control.

— David Hawkins

It can be said that the ego is a compilation of positionalities held together by vanity and fear. It is undone by radical humility.

— David Hawkins

All thoughts are vanities, with no intrinsic reality or value. Their attraction stems from the exaggerated value that accrues from their being considered as 'mine' and therefore special, worthy of respect, admiration, or careful preservation.

— David Hawkins

Ask for direction and divine assistance and surrender all personal will through devotion. Dedicate one's life to the service of God. Choose love and peace above all other options.

— David Hawkins

Your pain is the breaking of the shell that encloses your understanding...watch with serenity through the winters of your grief...trust the physician, and drink his remedy in silence and tranquillity.

— Kahlil Gibran

Every word is like an unnecessary stain on silence and nothingness.

— Samuel Beckett

Solitariness is a realized mode of being-in-the-world. Solitary man is always with God and with the world, at one with the universe. He does not use people to make himself feel good. He lives in the consciousness of the presence of omniactive Mind. Solitary man can be male or female, married or unmarried. Solitary man enjoys solitude, but he also enjoys company, and though he does not seek friends, he is very friendly. Truly, this is freedom and dominion.

— Thomas Hora

Silence is a source of Great Strength.

— Lao Tzu

A soul who has been given mastery of her own desire has a huge advantage. But she does not bequeath this dominion to herself. It is a gift from God.

— Teresa of Avila

It is a supreme joy to find myself living with such detached souls. All they talk about is how they can serve God better. They take comfort in solitude, and the only people they want to see are those who make the fire of their love for their beloved burn brighter. Otherwise, the thought of being with other people, even their own relatives, is a burden to them. They do not entertain idle visitors.

— Teresa of Avila

In the midst of this state of prayer, all thinking ceases. When I enter into that place, I can no longer think of a thing.

— Teresa of Avila

He who does not desire to be ahead of the world becomes the leader of the world.

— Lao Tzu

About the Author

Donna Goddard is an author and shares her love for the Divine and the world with a large international audience. She lives in Melbourne, Australia.

All links https://linktr.ee/donnagoddard

Love and Devotion - next book in series

Love and Devotion is a four-book nonfiction series. To find the great Love, we must, one way or another, die the great death. Once that death is conquered, we won't have to die again. There is a grand and magnificent truth that radiates from within all of life and each of us. May you discover in your heart a sweet lightness, the luminescent glow of God's beauty, and a true appreciation for the wonderful gift of life which glows unmarred through every human error. We are loved by the Divine, loved into existence. That, in itself, is enough to reassure each one of us of our inestimable worth.

The **next book,** in the series, is ***Love's Longing***. Somewhere along the way, there develops within the soul a yearning that can no longer be ignored; a craving for the great Love affair.

Acknowledgments

The author gratefully acknowledges Veritas Publishing for permission to use quotes from Dr David R. Hawkins, founder of the Institute of Advanced Spiritual Research, at www.veritaspub.com

Ratings and Reviews

I would be most grateful for any ratings or reviews.

Printed in Great Britain
by Amazon

78694971R00078